TRANSFORMING
PAIN
TO
POWER

TRANSFORMING
PAIN
TO
POWER

UNLOCK YOUR
UNLIMITED POTENTIAL

DANIEL BEATY

BERKLEY BOOKS, NEW YORK

THE BERKLEY PUBLISHING GROUP
Published by the Penguin Group
Penguin Group (USA) LLC
375 Hudson Street, New York, New York 10014

USA • Canada • UK • Ireland • Australia • New Zealand • India • South Africa • China

penguin.com

A Penguin Random House Company

This book is an original publication of The Berkley Publishing Group.

First Edition: March 2014

Library of Congress Cataloging-in-Publication Data

Beaty, Daniel.
Transforming pain to power : unlock your unlimited potential / by Daniel Beaty. — 1st Edition.
p. cm.
ISBN 978-0-425-26748-6
1. Self-actualization (Psychology)   2. Self-control.   I. Title.
BF637.S4B3953 2014
158—dc23   2013042635

PRINTED IN THE UNITED STATES OF AMERICA

10   9   8   7   6   5

Jacket design by Judith Lagerman
Jacket photograph © Josh Lehrer
Interior text design by Tiffany Estreicher

CONTENTS

FOREWORD

by Michael Eric Dyson

YOUR DAILY DOSE

Too many of us go a lifetime without coming to a critical insight: The painful experiences we endure can launch us to incredible futures. Sure, it sounds like one of the "um" family: pablum, perhaps hokum, maybe even a nostrum. But the hard, cold fact is that those folk who find the power to dig through the hurtful "no's" in their lives can find their way to a resounding "yes." That sounds like more self-help mumbo-jumbo still, but the truth is that we all need help, and the self is as good a place to start as any other; indeed, before any other.

Let's be honest: Too many of us haven't given ourselves—our *selves*—permission to heal. We barricade ourselves behind this theory or that fantasy of abstract, impersonal history and fail to grasp our role in making sure that we make it to wholeness. That scares some of us because we believe that it denies the vicious roll of blind social forces that target some folks and communities with unrelenting intensity. Not so!

There's no denying that no matter what you do with yourself—your self—that there are bigger factors at play that can set you on course, or knock you off-kilter, in the blink of an eye. The broader world can ever bring menace and misery to your door, true. But many of the people who've fought back against these larger forces, folks who've identified the social pathologies at the root of personal suffering, have at least acknowledged that we can take actions to make sure that things turn out better than they might if we just accept things, and ourselves—our selves—as we are.

As we fight against injustice, as we speak back to pain, as we argue with merchants of unnecessary grief, we must always, at the same time, fix up, as best we can, with what we have at hand and heart, the selves that will occupy the just society for which we struggle. The beauty of social justice is that it brings into sharper focus the care for self that is far more than either brutal narcissism or extravagant selfishness. We learn to embrace a better self as we struggle for a better world.

The great thing about our greatest artists and thinkers is that they help us put on bifocals to focus on the larger landscape of the social order and the intimate space of ourselves—our selves. When we listen to songs, read books, attend plays, see visual art and move to the rhythms of dance, we enlarge our understanding of the world around us, and the world teeming inside us. We learn many lessons from our artists, none more important than that the pain that dogs us can be put to great use if we can find a way to love ourselves—our selves—and beat back the forces that threaten to drag us down from outside or within.

Thank God for Daniel Beaty. He is a gifted and brave soul who is willing to share with you what he's learned from struggling against ugly odds to craft a life of fierce loyalty to truth while standing strong in the midst of heartbreak and humiliation. Long ago, like the legendary former UN Secretary-General Dag Harmmarskjöld, he said yes to his destiny and no to the forces that would take him down. The book you hold in your hand is an honest and searing road map to one man's wisdom of survival, and if you follow it, you might find that it helps you do the same thing. You can't ask much more of a book, and this book delivers with clarity, poetry, and power. Take it in daily doses. Use it at the risk of your improvement. Recognize that its side effects are deepened understanding and broad growth. And realize that before you know it, as you read about his transforming pain to power, you might do the same. There's nothing better that Beaty or any of us who admire his work could ever hope for.

Introduction

The Artist must elect to fight for
freedom or for slavery.
I have made my choice.
I had no alternative.

—PAUL ROBESON

I am an Artist who has chosen freedom over slavery, and my purpose is to empower others to do the same—to transform their pain to power. And by Artist I mean I am a creative being, as we all are, with the unlimited potential to be an active participant in the moment-to-moment creation of my life. Every breath is an opportunity to choose either freedom or slavery: We can choose to be overcome by the challenges that appear in our lives or we can choose to know and live in the *truth* of who we are. Regardless of our age, race, class, sex, sexuality, or any other label of identity, the *truth* is that at the core of us all is an AUTHENTIC SELF that is the unlimited potential to create, do, or be anything. The Authentic Self is greater than any difficult circumstances that may be in our past or present. The Authentic Self is greater than any resulting negative thoughts or feelings.

I grew up in Dayton, Ohio, in a home scarred by addiction and incarceration. For most of my childhood and early adult years, I thought chaos, bondage, and sadness were the norm. My father was a heroin addict and dealer and had spent most of my life in and out of prison. My older brother followed in my father's footsteps, becoming addicted to crack cocaine and spending time in prison as well. My concept of who I could be in the world was greatly influenced by the men in my home.

Then, when I was in the third grade, my teacher Mavis Jackson played Dr. King's "I Have a Dream" speech on videotape, and I saw a powerful image of another type of man I could be. This man was standing in front of tens of thousands of people using *words* to literally change the world—to open hearts and minds. I said to my teacher, "I want to use words like that!" And my life, in one form or another, has always followed that path.

Right away, my third grade teacher, Ms. Jackson, helped me to write my first speech, "I Think the Best, I Expect the Best." She then called local service organizations and clubs like Optimist International, Rotary, Kiwanis International, the NAACP, and the Southern Christian League, and said, "I have a third grade student who has written a powerful speech. Can he come to your local meeting and share?" All of the organizations agreed, and once I shared at the local clubs, the organizers would tell the club in the town over, then the state convention, then the national convention. Before I realized what was happening, I was traveling all over the country giving speeches. My "biggest hit" was a speech called "The Dream Is Alive" about all the ways Dr. King's dream had become a reality and all the work there was still to do. Looking back, I wonder what it must have been like for those adults to hear a child speaking of such lofty ideas about human transformation. But I also believe children have special lessons to teach us about possibility, imagination, and hope. And while we may now be "grown-ups," I invite you to embrace a childlike curiosity and openness in exploring the concepts in this book.

Eventually, I discovered the performing arts and found my home in dramatic form as a playwright and performer. I began to ask myself, "How can I tell a story that has the potential to make a deep impact—to change the world?" That's a big thought, isn't it? That a performance could change the world? But hey, it is the job of Artists to dream! I am interested in big questions because the world is full of big problems. Even in my dramatic writings, my purpose has always been to lead people toward transformation. And although my most public platform has been as a writer and performer, I have always been simultaneously working and honing my skills as a motivational speaker, workshop facilitator, and professor.

Simply put, people are suffering, and in this book, through memoir, poetry, character monologues, recovery technology, exercises, and statements of affirmation, I intend to share all that I have learned with the goal of empowering people to create the lives of their dreams.

As a little boy, my whole chaotic world began to shift because of my witnessing the power of Dr. King's "I Have a Dream" speech. Similarly, it is my intention—my dream—that readers who experience *Transforming Pain to Power* will be catapulted to breakthroughs beyond their wildest imaginings.

The concepts I will share in this book are a culmination of my studies at Yale University, American Conservatory Theater, my training and experience as a personal coach, and my training as an educator in some of the most economically challenged communities in New York City and beyond. And while I have studied complex theories at leading institutions, I have endeavored to distill these concepts in the simplest, clearest manner possible. I may have made my way to Yale, but that is not where I started. You will learn more about my beginnings throughout this book. It is important to me that these ideas are available and accessible to everyone. I have also refined and evaluated these concepts by studying various books on human transformation and comparative religion. I further developed these ideas by studying the human mind, body, breath, and meditation. Most importantly, these concepts are based on my personal journey to overcome an upbringing marked by addiction, incarceration, poverty, sadness, and rage to create a life I love.

My life has been graced with the appearance of ANGELS who have led me through moments of intense darkness and empowered me to realize my potential. Throughout this book, you will meet these Angels, and it is my hope that if I share stories of my experiences with them, their wings will cover you also and some of the grace I have experienced from them will be passed on to you.

If you have ever experienced pain in your life, this book is for you. If you have learned some healing and empowerment concepts, but still have areas in your life where you are endeavoring to overcome, this book is for you. While the recovery technology in this book is rooted in spiritual principles designed to transform a person's relationship to his or her thoughts and emotions, I will not put forth a particular spiritual or religious view, because these methods are compatible with all religions. And I use the words "recovery technology" very specifically. At the speed our lives are moving in our present society, with technological advances and overstimulation from media, we need tools that move, a recovery technology that moves, at the speed of our lives. I will delve into the concepts in a myriad of ways throughout the book, but the basic principle is simple: No matter who you are, where you are, or what you've been through, there is a power within you that is the unlimited potential to create, do, or be anything. How do you access this power? I invite you to turn the page and take this journey with me . . .

1

The Power of Pain

Pain doesn't last always
Sometimes only for a night
Try not to resist
It hurts the more we fight
The path is rocky and long
But in the end you'll be more strong
than you dreamed you'd be
Open your eyes and see:
Pain doesn't last always
Sometimes only for a night
Try not to resist
It hurts the more we fight

was almost born in prison. At the time of my conception my father was one of the most wanted heroin dealers in the nation. One afternoon, the cops broke into our home, and my mother, who was six months pregnant, was there—and so was the heroin. The judge gave my father a choice: he could either turn in the higher ranking members of his crew, or he and my mother could go to prison, which would cause me to be born in a prison hospital and my parents to remain incarcerated for years.

My father made the decision to be a "snitch," and although he and my mother were both set free (albeit, my father was only free for a short time), an inheritance of imprisonment was still passed on.

My entire life has been a journey to get free—to escape the chains that have kept me bound. In this book I am going to talk openly about my life and tell you a lot of my business. I just ask that you keep your heart and mind open to what I have to say. I am going to share with you moments when I thought I was unattractive, unworthy of love, incapable of being greater than the circumstances of disenfranchisement I inherited, even moments when I wanted to give it all up and end my life. And I'm also going to share with you how I got over. Or I should say, more accurately, how day by day.I continue the process of getting over—how day by day, sometimes moment by moment, I continue to heal, to grow, to create the life of my dreams, and ultimately to live a life of purpose that is about service to others. Somewhere along my journey I discovered that the only possibility I could ever have of getting free and of maintaining that freedom was to inspire that possibility in others. And somewhere along the journey I discovered that our deepest pain is often the path to our highest purpose. There is power in our pain. And this first chapter explores exactly that: the Power of Pain.

> ## Our deepest pain is often the path to our highest purpose.

No matter where you come from or where you are in this moment, you have within you the unlimited potential to create, do, or be anything. No matter the pain you have experienced in your past or may be experiencing in this very moment, you can transform that pain to power. You can live the life of your dreams.

No matter how many times you have been disappointed, no matter how many negative thoughts and emotions seem to keep you bound, you can be free. In fact, who you are is freedom. Who you are is unlimited. Who you are is more powerful than your greatest dreams. Can you believe it? Belief is a choice. And in this moment I challenge you to believe. My life is proof that with a choice to believe, a little bravery, a lot of diligence, and the right tools you can transform your pain to power.

We all have challenging experiences in our lives no matter what our race, sex, class, or age, and the question is how do we choose to be with these challenges? Do we allow ourselves to become defeated and overwhelmed by the negativity that appears in our lives, or do we use those experiences to make us stronger and ultimately tell the story of how we got over in an effort to help someone else?

My purpose in life is to inspire people to transform their pain to power. I am a creative being by nature and training, so this book will mirror that creativity. In the following pages I will impart my story and a series of core principles that empower me to overcome my past pain on a daily basis, access my unlimited potential, and create the life of my dreams. Through my own personal story, I am going to share a technology that has literally saved my life—that daily saves my life. I would not be so arrogant as to suggest that I've got it all figured out or that my life is perfect. In fact, each day when I awake, I have to make the decision to choose power over pain, to choose joy over sorrow, to choose purposeful, creative living over old, familiar patterns.

Through heartbreak to hope, I have developed a series of concepts and tools that empower me daily to make the choices that enable me to create the life of my dreams. It's been a journey, but today, I know the truth of who I am, and the work becomes choosing day by day, sometimes moment by moment, to live in that truth. My intention with this book is to cause you to break through to a discovery of your truest, deepest self and to provide you with the tools to successfully make the choice day by day, sometimes moment by moment, to live in that truth.

The concepts I will share in this book are rooted in the idea of the Authentic Self that is based on the following principles:

1. All human beings have inside of them a core Authentic Self regardless of their race, class, sex, sexuality, education, family structure, or any other label of identity.

2. This core Authentic Self is the unlimited potential to create, do, or be anything.

3. We all have past experiences that are a part of our story. We own our story. Our story does not own us. Our future possibilities do not have to be limited by our past experiences or even our present circumstances.

4. We have thoughts and feelings. We are not our thoughts and feelings. The Authentic Self is the parent to our thoughts and feelings. When we operate from our Authentic Self, we can

use our thoughts and emotions to create our reality rather than living a life that is shaped by negative thoughts and emotions that are the result of past experiences.

5. Every human being adopts a variety of roles in his or her life. These are costumes that one wears interchangeably. One woman in the course of a single day may play the role of a mother, a daughter, a wife, a friend, a business owner, etc. By connecting with our Authentic Self we can embrace whatever label of identity we choose that empowers us to accomplish our greatest dreams.

I firmly believe that the self-defeating thought patterns, the negative emotions, the inability to manifest new possibilities and dreams experienced by many people reflect a lack of connection with the Authentic Self. They result from the fear of believing in our unlimited potential because of a lifetime of disappointments, because of painful past experiences. Many people have so identified themselves with their painful past experiences that they cannot see themselves separate from those experiences. They have so identified with the negative thought patterns resulting from those experiences that they cannot see themselves separate from those thoughts. When we become connected with our Authentic Self, we can begin to *observe* our thoughts and emotions, rather than identifying with them. The moment we begin to observe our thoughts and feelings, we separate from them and enter a space where we begin to understand that we have thoughts and feelings, but they do not have us. We have the power to choose what we think and feel. We can then embrace our power to use our thoughts and emotions to create the quality of life we desire and that will lead us toward manifesting our goals and dreams. Have you ever found yourself feeling sad or angry all of a sudden? You may even be in the company of people you enjoy, at a place you love. Often, people have no tools to go inside and ask themselves, "Why am I feeling this way? What am I thinking that is causing me to feel this way?" Asking these questions is what I mean by observing. The moment we become curious about what we are thinking and feeling, we take back ownership over our thoughts and feelings. We remember that we have the right to determine if we choose to feel or think a certain way. Does thinking this way serve me? Does feeling this way help me create the quality of life I desire? Exercises will follow to help us practice this powerful technique.

> We have the power to choose
> what we think and feel.

Identifying with our thoughts and emotions is disconnecting from our Authentic Self because the moment we attach ourselves to our thoughts and emotions we are not fully present. Thoughts and emotions can only live in the realm of past experience. Thoughts and emotions evaluate our present and future through the lens of our past. They thereby limit our present and future by creating a barrier to full presence. In order to feel safe in the world, we often make assumptions about who a person is and how a situation will turn out from our past experiences. Can you see how limiting that can be? Each moment has creative potential and power. But if we only view what is in front of us based on what we expect (because of past hurt, loss, and disappointment), we will miss out on countless opportunities. When we are fully present, we are able to see things clearly, process information more thoroughly, and experience each moment as it really is, instead of what we assume it will be. I'm not suggesting that we deny what we have learned in the past, but we also don't want to limit ourselves and other people to our past experiences. Life is too unexpected and full of magic for us to do that.

> Your present and future are
> not limited to or defined by
> your past experiences.

At the core of transforming your pain to power is the discovery that your present and future are not limited to or defined by your past experiences or the resulting patterns of thoughts and emotions.

When we truly understand our Authentic Self, we discover that all of the labels of identity we embrace are merely costumes we can choose to wear through knowing the power of our Authentic Self. Who we truly are is the unlimited ability to create, do, or be *anything*.

By choosing to read this book you have taken the first step toward transforming your pain to power. The choice to continue, to consider new ideas, to push yourself beyond your comfort zone is up to you.

You are at a moment of choice. In fact, every breath you breathe is an opportunity to choose your life's direction, to believe again or perhaps for the first time, to dream anew. Regardless of the challenging experiences you may have gone through, regardless of the pain you may even be experiencing right now, you do have agency in your life. The choice is yours. I firmly believe we all have the power from moment to moment to choose who we will be, no matter what shows up in our lives.

The particular circumstances of my life and my growing up have caused me to view life in this way. Now, I told you I was going to share with you a lot of my business, so here goes. You already know the circumstances around my birth. Here's what happened next . . .

KNOCK KNOCK

As a boy I shared a game with my father.
We played it every morning 'til I was three.
He would knock knock on my door
And I'd pretend to be asleep 'til he got right next to the bed,
Then I would get up and jump into his arms.
Good morning Papa.
And my Papa, he would tell me that he loved me.

We shared a game . . . knock knock.
'Til the day the knock never came
And my mama takes me on a ride
Past cornfields, on this never-ending highway,
'Til we reach a place of high rusty gates
A confused little boy, I enter the building
Carried in my mama's arms . . . knock knock
We reach a room of windows and brown faces.
Behind one of the windows sits my father.
I jump out of my mama's arms and run joyously towards
 my papa
Only to be confronted by this window
I knock knock trying to break through the glass, trying to get
 to my father
I knock knock as my mama pulls me away before my papa
 even says a word.
And for years he has never said a word
And so years later I write these words for the little boy in me
Who still awaits his papa's knock:
Papa come home 'cause I miss you,
Miss you waking me in the mornings and telling me you
 love me.
Papa come home 'cause there's things I don't know
And I thought maybe you could teach me
How to shave, how to dribble a ball,
How to talk to a lady, walk like a man,
Papa come home 'cause I decided a while back

I want to be just like you, but I've forgotten who you are.
And years later a little boy cries and so I write these words
    and try to heal,
Try to father myself
And I dream up a father who says the words my father
    did not:
Dear Son, I'm sorry I never came home.
For every lesson I failed to teach, hear these words:
Shave in one direction with strong, deliberate strokes to
    avoid irritation.
Dribble the page with the brilliance of your ballpoint pen.
Walk like a god and your goddess will come to you.
No longer will I be there to knock on your door so you
    must learn to knock for yourself.
Knock knock down doors of racism and poverty I
    could not.
Knock knock on doors of opportunity
For the lost brilliance of the men who crowd these cells.
Knock knock with diligence for the sake of your children.
Knock knock for me, for as long as you are free—
These prison gates cannot contain my spirit;
The best of me still lives in you.
Knock knock with the knowledge that you are my son,
But you are not my choices.
Yes, we are our fathers' sons and daughters, but we are not
    their choices
For despite their absences we are still here.

Still alive . . .
Still breathing . . .
With the power to change this world one little boy and girl at
   a time—
Knock knock.
Who's there?
We are.

As you just read in that poem, I was extremely close to my father as a child. He was my principal caregiver while my mother spent her days as a social worker. He was the one who changed my diapers and carried me on his shoulders to the grocery store. He woke me up every morning with our private game.

But when I was three years old he was arrested. His guilt over being "a snitch" and turning in his friends so that he and my mother could go free caused him to start using the heroin he was once only selling. Life is energy and our choices have power. You can't sell poison to people without it coming back to haunt you. My father's ghost became his own heroin addiction, and his addiction caused him to become "sloppy" in his criminal activity and to make some reckless choices to feed his habit.

Throughout the course of my life my father has been arrested fifty-eight times. The arrest that impacted my life the most was the one I describe in my poem "Knock Knock." When I was a three-year-old boy, my mother took me to visit my father in prison, and he was behind a glass—I could not reach him. And he remained unreachable for most of my childhood—with the exception of the brief moments when he would reappear before being arrested again.

This experience was for me what I call an INITIAL BREAK-DOWN. An Initial Breakdown is a core painful childhood experience that fractures your ego and that causes you to feel unsafe and to question your self-worth.

When I was three years old, my primary caregiver—my father—abandoned me, and the safety of his physical and emotional presence was no longer available to me. The world as I had always known it was thrown out of order.

Children need to feel safe. They need to be held, told they are loved, and to have the consistency of loving parents and community support. Unfortunately, too many of our children are not afforded such a nurturing, embracing environment. The reality is that we all have experiences at a very early age that deeply challenge our self-concept.

Investigating, understanding, and embracing our deepest pain are the first steps on the path to transforming our pain to power. Your deepest pain is rooted in an Initial Breakdown—a core experience that shattered your world as a child. It may have caused you to feel unsafe or that you were unworthy of love. The Initial Breakdown wounds your self-concept—it punctures a hole in your identity through which seeps your confidence and your belief in yourself, and through which negative thoughts and feelings can enter. For some, this experience starts in the womb with a mother who is an addict and abuses a substance, or who is emotionally depressed, or who is in a physically or emotionally abusive relationship. For some it starts with not being held and kissed as a newborn. An Initial Breakdown might be abandonment by a loved one at an early age, as was the case with me, and with many children, as the statistics of absent fathers tell.

> Investigating, understanding, and embracing our deepest pain are the first steps on the path to transforming our pain to power.

An Initial Breakdown might be words of untruth about your physical appearance or intelligence that were spoken to you as a child. The list goes on and on. It seems an Initial Breakdown is inevitable, almost like a required initiation into what it means to be human. Even the most loving parents in the world cannot prevent this from happening. If the breakdown doesn't occur in the home, it might happen on the playground or in school. The reality is that we all have a parcel of pain. It starts at an early age and it impacts us deeply.

What was your Initial Breakdown? Do you come up with an answer right away? Perhaps you have buried it so deeply you cannot even begin to contemplate what it might be. Perhaps there is more than one instance that comes to mind. There are probably many painful childhood experiences we can all remember. But there is one core experience that impacted you so deeply that even to this day you might be living out of the pain of that experience without even realizing it. At the end of this chapter I will lead you through an exercise to help you recognize an Initial Breakdown, but first let me unpack this a little further by introducing a few more concepts and sharing more of my personal story.

An Initial Breakdown creates a RESULTING THOUGHT PATTERN. The Resulting Thought Pattern is a central, negative self-defining thought that emerges from an Initial Breakdown.

My father abandoned me so I must not be good enough to be loved.

From the moment my father stopped waking me up in the morning with our "knock knock" game, and then through the difficult experience of visiting my father in prison and not being able to reach him because he was behind glass, I developed a private shame. I persistently had the thought that something must be terribly wrong with me if my father would leave me. That must be the reason, right? Or so I thought as a child. As children we are limited in our ability to process the complexities of life. We

24

are self-focused and view the world in terms of our most basic needs, and when those needs are not met the first conclusion we reach is that we are somehow responsible. As a child I needed my father to be there. I needed him to hold me and tell me I was strong and smart and to teach me how to become a man. And for me, what made it worse was that he had been there and then he left. What did I do wrong? I must have made him mad. I must have been bad. I must *be* bad because my father left me. I am bad and I hope nobody ever finds out. Thus began the private shame of my secret pain.

Even to this day, during moments of disappointment and frustration, when life doesn't work out the way I want it to, versions of these same negative thoughts start screaming in the recesses of my mind. "See, things didn't work out because I am bad and 'they' must have found out."

Sure, there is a great deal of complexity here that we could delve into, but I am keeping it simple to make a point. I am more interested in imparting the tools to transform our pain to power than I am in meandering endlessly through the maze and confusion of past pain. That said, understanding the most basic roots of our pain is a crucial step.

The Resulting Thought Pattern creates the DOMINATING EMOTIONAL LANDSCAPE. The Dominating Emotional Landscape consists of the primary negative emotions one feels rooted to in an Initial Breakdown and Resulting Thought Pattern.

Because my father abandoned me and I have the persistent thought that I am not good enough to be loved, I feel lonely, sad, insecure, and afraid. I feel unlovable.

Simply expressed: negative thoughts lead to negative feelings. If you are feeling badly, examine what you are thinking, and that will inevitably be the root. We will delve further into the power of our thoughts and emotions in future chapters, but what is important to understand in this moment is that a root childhood experience and the resulting negative thoughts can create an internal emotional landscape that can have a lasting impact on one's life.

Negative thoughts lead to negative feelings.

For as long as I can remember, I felt alone and unlovable. Today, I understand without a shadow of a doubt that this was the Dominating Emotional Landscape I developed as the result of my childhood abandonment by my father. I remember an exercise in an acting course at Yale in which I was asked to think of the person who loved me the most. I remember sitting for several moments completely unable to think of anyone who I believed loved me. Ultimately, I thought of a dog I had as a child. Surely, my dog loved me. Sounds pretty pathetic, right? Daniel was never loved by anyone but his dog! Now, I do believe pets can be a source of unconditional love, and that love can be unbelievably healing. But the reality is there was plenty of love in my life. My mother loved me. She didn't always express that love with hugs and kisses and words of affection, but she provided for me, and she exhausted herself to do so. I began to do motivational speaking at a very young age and had a whole community of people who expressed love toward me in my hometown of Dayton, Ohio. And I had teachers and friends and people at church who certainly loved me. But the reality is I did not truly feel this love, because I did not feel I was lovable. How can you receive what you don't believe you are worthy of? The result was that these negative thoughts and feelings had a profound impact on my behavior.

The Resulting Thought Pattern and the Dominating Emotional Landscape combine to create the RESULTING BEHAVIOR PATTERN. The Resulting Behavior Pattern is the primary, out-of-balance way one operates in the world, which is rooted in the negative Resulting Thought Pattern and the Dominating Emotional Landscape that have emerged from an Initial Breakdown. Try as one might, ultimately the Resulting Behavior Pattern can never be greater than the wound created by an Initial Breakdown.

I will overachieve to the point of exhaustion to prove to myself that I am worthy of being loved. When high achievement never heals the wound, I will still be in pain and feel like a failure.

Consider these words from the character Jessica in my musical *Tearing Down the Walls*. Her poem clarifies how her Initial Breakdown has resulted in a destructive Resulting Behavior Pattern.

What You Don't Know Can Hurt You

Is it a crime that I flaunt my sexuality?
And with a glance of my eyes draw men to me?
Oh, men have been staring before they should
A pretty little girl, I did everything I could to keep them
*   away,*
But there's a price you pay when you're pretty.
And so I learned to be witty and catch them off guard
Oh, I go hard but I do it in disguise
Oh, you'd have to be wise to catch my game
And it's a shame
I'll give you a taste, then leave you sad and blue
'Cause what you don't know can hurt you
See, men have been staring before they should
And a pretty little girl, I did everything I could to keep
*   them away*
But there's a price you pay when you're pretty—
He was much older, suave, and cool,
And I was a fool,
A young girl I should have been in school.

But he had nice things, fancy cars, diamond rings,
Promised if I'd be his girl he'd give me wings,
And I like to fly.
And that's why time and time again I gave him all of me
And he raped my innocence, my purity
And when he was done, did away with me.
I never did fly.
But I got high and I was high for years,
And it's been hell getting down.
So, I keep a man around,
But now I'm in control,
They get my body not my soul.
Yes, I wear this cape of sexuality
Like a Venus flytrap draw my prey to me.
Make you want me so much
Make you quiver at my touch
Give you the best lay of your life
Crying, "Baby, be my wife!"
Taking it all without a clue
That once you're mine, I'll be done with you.
And you'll be left looking sad and blue.
What you don't know can hurt you.

In the poem, Jessica has been so wounded by the sexual and emotional abuse she experienced from men as a child that she has adopted a behavior pattern of being a sexual and emotional abuser herself. Hurting people hurt people. Rather than embracing her pain so that she might heal, she has become the embodiment of pain.

EMBRACING THE PAIN

I am sick and tired of being sick and tired! I'm sick and tired of all these negatives thoughts. I don't want to feel this way anymore. I can't take it anymore! Have you ever had these thoughts and feelings? I know I have.

That which we resist persists. There comes a time when we must embrace the pain instead of attempting to resist it or pretending that the pain is not there or living with the effects of the pain without truly investigating its root. There comes a time when we must go in to come out. We must become real about our pain so that we may discover that it truly does not have power over us.

Running from your past
You stumble to your future.
Running from your past
Afraid of what is there.
Running from your past
You live the lie that makes it possible
To push beyond your fears—
Running from your past:
The way that you survived—

Running from your past
You hurry through your moments
Running from your past
You really aren't alive
Running from your past
You live the lie that robs you of true joy
Running from your past:
It's no way to survive.

I missed so much joy in my life running from my past—trying to hide my secret pain from other people and mostly from myself. This hiding from my pain had severe consequences for me. First and foremost, it caused me to live my life with a persistent sadness that permeated even those moments that should have been the most joyous. At my graduation from Yale University I received one of the three highest honors awarded to an undergraduate, and as I stood in front of thousands of people to be honored, I felt deeply sad inside. I have achieved many great things, but none of those achievements were able to heal the pain of my Initial Breakdown caused by the abandonment by my father.

That which we resist persists.

I remember saying to my mother in my early twenties, "I don't think I will ever be happy. I've been sad all my life." There were times when my secret pain caused me to abuse sex. I moved out of a whole borough of New York City because I was having too much sex! My secret pain caused me to abuse my body with food, eating to suppress the negative thoughts and emotions, yo-yoing fifteen to twenty pounds every few months despite working out like a madman to stay in shape. As I stated earlier, the predominant way I personally tried to hide my pain was through achievement and working myself to utter exhaustion. Because of the model of addiction in my family, I avoided going overboard abusing drugs and alcohol, but there were even times when I used alcohol and marijuana as an insufficient salve for my secret pain. I am not making a judgment call on how anyone chooses to live his or her life, but I am trying to be real here. And I am not talking about recreational pleasures that an adult may choose to engage in or not. What I am speaking of is an imbalance—abusing one's self in an effort to avoid pain. In my work, I see so many people who allow their pain to suffocate their possibility, and if being real about my journey can help someone, I am willing. What is the value of hiding, especially from yourself?

In my comedic family musical *Trippin'*, there is a character named Worm Book. He is a bookworm (literally a worm) with two learning disabilities—dyslexia and attention deficit disorder (ADD). He is slowly, but persistently trying to get to class at Columbia. Listen to his story.

I've got Dyslexia and ADD.
How jumbled can one mind be?

Life makes no sense to me.
That's why I study philosophy.
Maybe the great thinkers can help me see
Why life can be full of so much misery
And just today the answer came to me:
Life is the mess it's supposed to be.
It's hard for you and it's hard for me:
We all got issues. We all got issues.
Knowing life is hard is just the start.
I haven't shared with you the other part:
If life's hard for you and it's hard for me,
Why sit around and have a pity party?
We all got issues.
Feeling sad about your life and you wanna cry?
At least, it's not as bad as that other guy:
He's really got issues.
When ADD is getting me down.
All I have to do is look around.
We all got issues. Yeah, we all got issues.

We all got issues! There's really no use in pretending. Even if you are going to lie to everyone else, at least be real with yourself. It is impossible to avoid the pain forever, so we might as well embrace it. The following exercise is an opportunity to choose to be real with yourself and embrace the power of pain as an essential first step in transforming your pain to power.

———

EXERCISE:

Embracing the Power of Pain

1. Find a quiet place where you can have at least thirty minutes of uninterrupted time. Go to a place where you feel most safe and at peace. Perhaps it is a favorite room in your home. Maybe it's a nearby park or the library. Take a notebook and pen with you. Turn off your cell phone and find a comfortable place to sit. Sit so you can feel both of your feet on the ground. Allow your feet to stretch wide in your shoes from your toes to your heel. Perhaps even take off your shoes. Allow yourself to really sit on the seat (or the floor, if that's what you choose). Feel your buttocks melting into the surface. Allow your back to rest on the chair (or bench or tree or rock if you're seated in the park). Give yourself over to the seat and allow yourself to be held by it. Rest your hands loosely on your lap with your palms on your stomach. Allow your belly to be free. Allow your lips to be slightly parted and release any tension in your jaw by imagining you have cotton balls between your back upper and lower teeth. Close your eyes and take three cleansing breaths in through your nose and out through your mouth, breathing deeply into your belly. As you continue to breathe deeply, allow your mind to wander for a few moments to your childhood. Think back to some of your most painful and defining memories. Try not to force the memories. Just allow them to flow in

and out of your mind. Allow yourself to visualize them. Where were you? What time of year was it? What are the sounds, the smells? Give yourself a good five minutes to allow yourself to remember your childhood. If your mind wanders, reconnect with three cleansing breaths in through the nose and out through the mouth. And reconnect to your intention of allowing these memories to flood in.

2. Now open your notebook and write freely, in one-sentence memories, each of the experiences you remember. Some of my one-sentence memories would be:

a. *My father left when I was three and did not come home.*

b. *My mother was sad and stopped smiling at me.*

c. *My mother started yelling at me very loudly when I did something wrong.*

d. *I waited each morning, but my father never returned to play our knock knock game.*

3. Now examine these one-sentence memories. Which of them feels the most "heated" to you? Which of them has the most "emotional charge"? If more than one resonates with you deeply, what is similar about them and which happened first? Don't worry if you feel conflicted. Trust your instincts and choose one. This will serve as your Initial Breakdown for the

purposes of our work together. If at any point, you would like to choose a different experience, feel free. As we progress throughout the book, you will discover that the experience you choose is less important than how you choose to be with the resulting thoughts and feelings. Just choose one. See, we are already practicing our power of choice and agency in our lives—in how we respond to our pain.

4. Now that you have chosen your Initial Breakdown, once again close your eyes, place your hands on your stomach, and take three cleansing breaths in through your nose and out through your mouth. Allow yourself to meditate on the memory of this experience.

5. What are some of the thoughts that emerged from this experience? Again, in one-sentence statements write down any *thoughts* that came to you.

   a. *I thought I had done something wrong and that I was bad.*

   b. *I thought my father didn't love me anymore.*

6. What are some of the feelings that emerged from this experience? Again, in one-sentence statements write down any *feelings* that came to you.

   a. *I felt ashamed and unlovable.*

   b. *I felt alone.*

7. Turn to a blank sheet of paper and start a journal entry that begins, "Dear Self," and write to yourself any current behaviors you can think of that you believe might be connected to this Initial Breakdown and the resulting negative thoughts and emotions. Be real with yourself.

   a. *I look in the mirror and I don't like what I see.*

   b. *In a relationship, when things go wrong, I leave before the other person leaves me because I think/feel it is inevitable that they will leave me.*

   c. *I feel ashamed and unworthy of love so I abuse my body with sex, drugs, or alcohol.*

   d. *When I wake up in the morning I feel sad or angry or numb.*

8. Find a mirror and speak to yourself the Statements of Affirmation at the end of this chapter. For some people this step may seem corny and unnecessary or feel uncomfortable and weird, but I promise you, it works. Speaking these affirmations to myself in front of a mirror has drastically changed my self-concept. As a child, I was darker in complexion than the other members of my family and had full lips, a wide nose, a big butt, a gap in my center front teeth, and a lazy eye. I was repeatedly teased and called names by family members and people in the community. I hated my features. I hated my dark skin. On a very basic level I hated myself. When I discovered the power of Affirmative Speaking (which

we will delve into more in a later chapter), I began to speak truth to those lies and it was a crucial step in my journey to self-love, acceptance, and celebration of the unique value and beauty that every single human being possesses.

If you have fully committed to the steps of the exercise above, you have done very deep emotional work, and it is imperative that you remind yourself of your intention in delving into these memories and honor the mental and emotional impact the process can have on you. With clarity and boldness speak the following words. Say them until you believe them, and if you are unable to arrive at the place of belief, fake it till you make it. Sometimes we have to speak those things that are not as though they were!

STATEMENTS OF AFFIRMATION

- ✦ I have thoughts and I have feelings, but I am not my thoughts and I am not my feelings.

- ✦ I have some painful past experiences, but I choose not to be limited by those experiences.

- ✦ I have agency and power in my life.

- ✦ I am proclaiming my ability to transform my pain to power.

- ✦ I understand that in the process of my healing, some negative, painful experiences and memories will emerge.

✦ I allow the space for my thoughts and feelings even though they may be painful, because I know that my intention is to create the life of my dreams.

✦ Even though I may not think or feel it in this moment, I boldly proclaim:

- *I am powerful!*

- *I am greater than my past!*

- *I am greater than any negative thoughts or feelings!*

- *I choose to be gentle, patient, and loving with myself.*

- *I am worthy of peace and joy.*

- *I am worthy of my dreams.*

2

The Power of Breath and Your Authentic Self

Take me to a place where there is no more pain
To a place where flowers consume all the rain
No more flooding—make it cease
Take me to a place, a place of peace
Come save me before I drown,
I'm floating down, down, down,
Come save me before I drown
I'm floating down
Take me to a place where there is no more pain

Three A.M. I awake in my dorm room gasping for breath. I grasp ahold of my sheets attempting unsuccessfully to lift my body. I can't breathe. It feels as though a four-hundred-pound demon is standing on my chest and grabbing me by my throat. I let out a scream from the depths of my belly and that scream floods into tears. Breath. Tears. More breath, more tears.

Before falling asleep, I remember thinking, *I can't do this anymore. I don't want to be alive anymore. Maybe the only way I can stop this pain is to end my life. Where can I get some pills? Or maybe I should just climb to the top of Harkness Tower* [the largest building on campus] *and jump from there.*

To those who knew me, this flood of negative thoughts and emotions would have seemed absurd. Here I was a sophomore at

Yale University, receiving excellent grades, performing in plays, giving concerts of classical music. Even at this young age, I had won numerous scholarships and awards. Growing up in a household with issues of addiction, poverty, and incarceration, I threw myself into achievement. In some ways, I was running from feelings of insecurity and in search of external validation, and for a time, this served me well. I was by most people's definition a success.

But in my own heart I felt like a failure and a fraud. And I was terrified that at any moment I was going to be found out and kicked off campus.

The depth of pain I felt that evening was the beginning of what I call my HEALING JOURNEY. And for me, it started with breath. The medical term for what I experienced that night was panic attack. But more than that, the experience of losing my breath signified to me how desperately I needed to connect to my breath—to breathe in life, to *choose* to be present.

In my studies as an actor and singer, I had been taught that emotion and power are rooted in the breath, but I had not considered what this might mean for my life outside of performance. I would take a singing lesson or an acting class and feel such freedom. Then I would retreat back into the bondage of my negative thoughts and feelings without realizing that the same freedom I had just experienced performing was continually available to me if I could just remember to breathe.

Try it now. Take three cleansing breathes in through your

nose and out through your mouth. With each inhale choose to be present in this very moment. With each exhale choose to release any thoughts or feelings that inhibit your full concentration on your breath. This simple act of noticing your breath and choosing to be present with your inhale and exhale is bringing you powerfully into *this moment*—not the past, not the future.

In this moment, in this breath, there is nothing wrong. There is nothing to be fixed or altered. This moment, this breath, is connected with your Authentic Self, and from this space you can cease to identify with your thoughts and feelings, begin to notice them, and *choose* how to be with them.

Perhaps a thought has emerged because it needs contemplation. Perhaps an emotion has arisen to reveal something that needs to be explored. More often than not, these persistent negative thoughts and feelings are the unconscious anxiety that has pervaded too much of human existence. More often than not, this anxiety is based in past experiences or future worries. But the truth is, the past has already happened, and the best way to create the future of your dreams is to honor this very moment right now—this breath.

The Power of Breath is the first step to beginning to observe one's thoughts and feelings. In this chapter, I will share with you a breathing and meditation exercise that will enable you to observe your thoughts and emotions. When you observe your thoughts and emotions, you are connected with your Authentic Self. The Observer *is* the Authentic Self. Your thoughts and emotions are the children of your Authentic Self. They must be observed, listened to, given boundaries, and trained to be healthy, productive, loving participants in your life.

The Power of Breath is the first step to beginning to observe one's thoughts and feelings.

Think of the children in your life. Imagine how they would behave with no boundaries. Imagine how they might process information without a loving, mature adult to explain to them why a person may have responded to them a certain way or why something didn't happen the way they desired. It is the job of parents and other loving adults to provide children with the necessary information and tools they need to have wonderful lives. Similarly, it is the job of the Authentic Self to speak to our thoughts and feelings so that we can create wonderful lives.

It's hard to tell yourself not to have a certain thought or feeling. It's like someone asking you not to think of a pink elephant, and of course, all you can think of is a pink elephant. It is more effective to *observe* what you are thinking and feeling, and then *choose* a thought that empowers you. For example, if you put on an outfit, look in the mirror, and think, *I've put on a couple of pounds. I look fat in this.* Depending on who you are this thought may stay with you as you finish getting dressed, once you get in the car, through dinner, when you take off your clothes at night, and when you lie down to go to sleep. This is how insistent and out of control our minds can be. You may tell yourself throughout the evening, *Stop thinking that way! Stop being so hard on yourself.* And, inevitably the thought reappears. For some, this type of negative self-talk can put a damper of their self-confidence and potentially ruin their evening. Telling yourself to stop thinking you look fat will not work for most people. But breathing, observing what you are thinking about yourself, contemplating the impact it is having on you (*this makes me feel horrible*), and then choosing empowering thoughts—*I look beautiful, my body is wonderful just as it is, more of me to love*, or whatever works for you—works to transform your thoughts and feelings. I am not suggesting the negative thoughts won't come back, but this is a tool to empower you immediately. Remember, we are talking about "recovery technology"—tools that move at the speed of our lives and our modern day world. Each time the negative thought appears, feed yourself a positive one.

The Observer is the Authentic Self.

The following exercise will allow us to begin to practice observing our thought and feelings, a first and crucial step in owning our power to be creative forces in our lives.

EXERCISE:
Checking In

1. Find a quiet place where you have at least fifteen minutes of uninterrupted time. Go to a place where you feel most safe and at peace. Perhaps it is a favorite room in your home. Maybe it's a nearby park, or even a library. Shut off your cell phone so you have no interruptions, and find a comfortable place to sit. Sit so you can feel both of your feet on the ground. Allow your feet to stretch wide in your shoes from your toes to your heels. Perhaps even take your shoes off. Allow yourself to really sit on the seat. Feel your buttocks melting into the surface. Allow your back to rest on the chair (or bench or tree or rock, if you are sitting in a park). Give yourself over to the seat and allow yourself to be held by it. Rest your hands loosely on your lap with your palms on your stomach. Allow your belly to be free. Allow your lips to be slightly parted and release any tension in your jaw by imagining you have cotton balls between your back upper and lower teeth. Close your eyes and take three cleansing breaths in through your nose and out through your mouth, breathing deeply into your belly.

2. What dominant thoughts are you having right now in this moment? How are you feeling right now in this moment? Allow yourself to simply observe your thoughts and emotions.

Try not to judge them or to fix them. If your mind attempts to wander, simply bring your attention back to your hands resting on your stomach, to the freedom of your belly, and to the easy inhalation through your nose and exhalation through your mouth.

The very act of observing your thoughts from your breath begins the discovery of your Authentic Self. The Observer is the Authentic Self.

LABELS OF IDENTITY

All of the labels of identity we embrace are merely costumes that cover our Authentic Self. Knowledge of our Authentic Self allows us to become conscious of our ability to choose, transform, or shift how we identify in the world. We can still choose to wear whatever costume we desire. I can wear the costume of urban swag when I desire, and I can wear the costume of corporate professionalism when I desire.

Every human being adopts a variety of roles in his or her life. These are costumes that one wears interchangeably and sometimes simultaneously. In the course of a single day you may play the role of a friend, a brother, a son, a student, an employee, etc. Different costumes are appropriate for different environments.

EXERCISE:
The Roles We Play

Please take out your notebook and answer the following questions:

1. What are the various roles you play throughout the course of a single day?

2. What does each particular person/environment need from you?

3. What part of yourself, your abilities, do you access to fulfill the needs of each particular person/environment?

> The Authentic Self is an agent
> of transformation that empowers
> you to be whomever you
> choose to be.

The purpose of this exercise is to cause you to discover that on a daily basis you already play a myriad of roles in life. Still you are not defined or limited by any one of those roles. These various roles combine to make up your identity. The question becomes, "If I am playing all these roles, who or what is the force that enables me to shift, to transform as needed?" That force is the Authentic Self. The Authentic Self is an agent of transformation that empowers you to be whomever you choose to be.

I invite you to consider the following comedic words of the character Anton from my play *Emergency*. Anton is a Jamaican man who has fully embraced the power of his Authentic Self and his ability to transform his identity—perhaps to the extreme. You be the judge. He has just learned about a slave ship that has magically arisen in front of the Statue of Liberty in present day New York City, and someone asks him if he is going to go see it.

No, man, me ain't goin' go see it.
Me don't need go Liberty Island to see no slave ship.
All me need do is look around this park.
Yeh man, we all got a slave ship . . . here . . . in the mind
And we're all bound up,
Sailing around in our slave ships thinking this bullshit world
*   reality*
When all we need to do is jump overboard into our Spirit.
Freedom . . . it's got nothing to do with society.
Freedom . . . it's about the mind.
'Bout taking control of your slave ship and steering it
*   home . . . to the truth of who you are. And that truth, it*
*   whoever you think you are.*
Take me for example. Me a white man. Me decided last
*   year.*
Think about it . . . when we die everything wastes away . . .
*   but the bones.*

Time passes and the casket . . . it's full of bones.
Check this: we all got white bones.
We all the same on the inside, so why can't me be a white
  man on the outside?
It's all about freedom. Liberate your mind . . .
Me don't have no job because everyone think me crazy—
When me check the box marked white on the application.
Me girlfriend, she say me lazy, me don't wanna do no work.
Me say, "Me a rich white man.
Me jus' waitin' for the Universe to notify the bank."

Clearly, the basis of this monologue is comedic, and I'm not sure Anton's philosophy is working for him, or that it would work for anyone else. Still, he underscores some important distinctions between being bound by thoughts of the mind—which he compares to a slave ship—and jumping overboard into the spirit, which for our purposes we would define as the Authentic Self. Anton is suggesting that beyond the limitations of our thoughts, there is a place in our Authentic Self where we are unlimited. And by accessing this space we can obtain a level of unexpected and empowering freedom.

Sometimes in my creative work as a performer, I work on pieces in which I play multiple characters, requiring me to memorize large amounts of dialogue and master several different personality types. Some of the shows last two hours, and I portray more than forty different roles. When I am presenting a new work in front of an audience for the first time, many negative thoughts run through my head: The dominating emotion is fear. The costume I am wearing is the Insecure Actor. So what I do is observe what I am thinking and feeling. Then, I feed myself new thoughts and don a new costume. *What is my purpose here? What can I give to the people gathered in this audience? I can inspire them with my bravery and creativity. I can be so committed and bold that people discover something new for themselves.* The costume I am wearing then is the Artist/Healer.

The character of Anton is intentionally over-the-top, but I use it to make a strong point. Our thoughts and feelings can keep us captive like slaves. Out of control, negative thoughts and feelings can rob us of our freedom, our joy, and our ability to create extraordinary lives. What we all need to do is jump overboard . . . jump into our Authentic Self . . . be free to be whoever we choose to be.

STATEMENTS OF AFFIRMATION

- ✦ My breath is the gateway to my Authentic Self.

- ✦ And through this gateway is a realm of unlimited possibilities.

- ✦ I play a myriad of roles in my life, but I do not have to be limited or defined by any of those roles.

- ✦ Through the power of my Authentic Self I remember:

  - • I have agency and power in my life.

- I am proclaiming my ability to transform my pain to power.

◆ Through my breath I access my Authentic Self and I proclaim:

  - *I am powerful!*

  - *I am greater than my past!*

  - *I am greater than any negative thoughts or feelings!*

  - *I choose to be gentle, patient, and loving with myself.*

  - *I am worthy of peace and joy.*

  - *I am worthy of my dreams.*

3

The Power of Your Thoughts and Your Mental Inheritance

December 1995. It is Christmas break during my sopho-more year of college. I'm back home in Dayton, Ohio, and I've decided to do it. I'm going to visit my father in prison. This will be the first time I have seen my father in more years than I can remember—at least ten. As I ride in the car next to my mother, all manner of thoughts and emotions course through me. *Do I look like him? What if he doesn't like me? What if I don't like him?*

I arrive at the prison, a massive gray and brown industrial complex. A large, muscular, imposing guard stands at the counter as I enter the first door.

Take everything out of your pockets and place it in that basket.

I do as I am instructed, terrified. As I remove my keys and wallet from my pocket, I can feel the sweatiness of my palms. The guard presses a buzzer. Buzz. A gate opens.

Enter through here.

Gate one. Slam. Buzz. Another gate opens. Gate two. Slam. I enter a room of tables and brown faces. Men with their children, girlfriends, mothers, wives sit not touching but with a longing to touch pouring from their eyes. Some of the men are chained around their ankles, some also around their wrists—but most have hands that are free.

Anxiously, I stare in the direction from which I see the men arriving and departing. I feel my heart beating in my throat, and I swallow hard, eager and afraid to see my father. He enters wearing a bright orange jumpsuit; he has salt-and-pepper hair and is much older than I remember. The guard removes the chains around his ankles, around his wrists. Thank God. He walks slowly toward me and opens his arms. And I jump. *Knock Knock.*

In this moment, I am once again the little boy that longed for his daddy. In this moment, all the love I felt for him as a small child comes flooding back to me. As I sit and listen to his stories—some certainly lies and excuses—I devour every word, desperate for them to be true, desperate to understand, to believe that his choices, his abandonment were not my fault.

The layers and complexities of my emotions will come later—

rage, sadness, grief for time lost, accountability, truth. But in this initial visit, the dominant feeling is love.

After this visit with my father we write letters back and forth over a period of several months, to begin the process of healing our relationship. This letter exchange enabled me to develop the concept of a MENTAL INHERITANCE.

Your MENTAL INHERITANCE consists of the primary thought patterns you inherited/learned from your primary caregiver(s) and core community as a child, through both conscious and unconscious suggestion.

Inheritance can be more than houses, land, money, and physical traits. One can also inherit patterns of thinking and emotional behavior.

Because my father was not present in my life growing up, I did not learn the ways he thought by observing him. For me, this Mental Inheritance came through letters in which he imparted to me his patterns of thought. Allow me to share with you excerpts from two letters to illustrate my point.

The first pattern of thought I learned from my father was something he called "the Con." The following is a direct quote from one of his letters to me in early spring 1996.

At all times, you must figure out who you need to be for people to get what you want from them. Everybody needs you to be someone, and once you figure out who that is, adopt that persona, and then act the role so well you get lost in your own lie. "The Con": it's what the greatest CEO's do, it's what the greatest con men do—same difference. Used correctly, and in promotion of self, "the Con" can take you a long way. I'm talking about real life, Danny, life the way it really is. You must manipulate past every obstacle. If you encounter resistance, don't fight, don't run, don't quit, and don't cry. Simply change the role you're playing. That's "the Con."

And here is an excerpt from another letter later that spring.

If you are not running "the con," you need a good dose of "'Arrogance." Without arrogance, people would not be the survivors they are. What arrogance does for people is simple: it lets them feel their power. It constantly recharges their self-esteem. Mainly, it repels the negative. I am talking about the difference between a beggar and the beggar with majestic bearing. They are different—one simply is and one is proud to be; one is merely a beggar and one is arrogant—I may be a beggar, but I still have tremendous value as a human being. It doesn't matter what social status we possess, what we feel inside, really feel inside, is our appearance to the world. A person will always see what's inside of us. And that is why "Arrogance" is essential: knowing that whatever life presents you, you can conquer it. No matter what your mind tells you, you are greater. I will never allow my own mind to dic-

tate whether I am happy. My well-being will always depend on my power to choose. "Arrogance." I am talking about street smarts, son, something traditional education will never teach. I have experienced life to such an extreme that there have been times when I didn't know if I would be killed or if I would have to kill. I had to be clear I could handle anything to survive. That is the lesson of "Arrogance."

These powerful and complex words of wisdom are part of my Mental Inheritance from my father. He shared these words with me while I was at the beginning of my Healing Journey, in deep pain and confusion. These words came from my father, a man who had been battling a heroin addiction for nearly two decades at this point, had been arrested fifty-eight times, and was serving an eight-and-a-half-year sentence in prison. Though his language and choice of action are different, he is essentially speaking of the power of the Authentic Self—our ability to *choose* how we think, feel, and exist in the world.

When I read these words now, on the upside of my Healing Journey, the wisdom they display is mind-boggling to me. My father understands principles of success in a profound way; he just chose a destructive path to express them. I wonder what my life might have been like had I seen him model these powerful thought patterns in a productive way. I wonder what I might have *inherited* by the model of his living, thinking, and making positive choices in front of me and then explaining to me the "reasoning" behind those choices.

YOU ARE NOT YOUR THOUGHTS

Do you have thoughts or do your thoughts have you? You have thoughts, but you are not your thoughts. With every breath, you can make the choice from your Authentic Self to discard thoughts that do not serve you and to choose thoughts that empower you.

The following excerpt from my play *Through the Night* underscores the power of our thoughts as well as explores an effective way to respond to negative thoughts when they emerge. The speaker is named 'Twon. He has grown up in a poor community—the projects. His father is incarcerated and has been absent from his life for most of his growing up. 'Twon is dyslexic, and because of a challenged school system, his teachers did not identify it immediately. But through the help of a mentor, he is graduating from high school and on his way to Morehouse—the same school Dr. King attended. But despite how far he has come, he still wrestles with doubt and fear. As you read this poem, I would like for you to consider the aspect of negative self-talk—the emotions of doubt and fear—that may be showing up in your own life.

> You have thoughts, but you are
> not your thoughts.

Run Black Man Run

I've been told—every action begins with a thought.
And if you don't watch what you're thinking, your
    thoughts will get the best of you.
It's like the Mind is an untrained child, you have to teach
    what to do—
'Cause sometimes my Mind, he tells me . . .
You will never be enough—
Why even try when you know it's gon' be tough?
Look at where you live, broken hopes and broken dreams,
At night you lie in bed and scream the silent scream
Of the bastard child without a father as a guide,
Sure Mama's there, but there's no Daddy by your side,
And so you push your cries away and fill that space
    with rage,
A rage that keeps you caged in a cycle that never ends:
Your Daddy left so you will too—
You ain't gon' be no better than the man who fathered you—
Able to create life, but not to follow through,
The sins of the father will visit the son,
When life gets tough, the abandoned run
So sag your pants and wear a frown,
Give up first before life tears you down.
Run from dreams and run from hope,
It's the only way to cope with the failure you will be,

A spitting image of the father you will never even see.
These are the thoughts my Mind, he says to me
Trying to choke out any type of hope or possibility
And that's why I delve into the depths of me and talk
    back to my Mind—
All right, I've heard enough, I know my path is rough,
But my Mama she was there and she helped me to prepare
A father she was not, but still she gave me a lot,
I will not let you say whatever you want;
I am determined to make it through
Because I define my destiny,
I won't let doubt get the best of me—
I will father myself so my children will see—
A Black Man stays,
This can be just a phase,
This cycle can end,
It all depends on where we go from here.
You say when life gets tough the abandoned run,
Well I say run Black Man run—
Run to your children—hold them tight,
Help them make it through the night,
Be more than you think you can,
Be a Black Man—take a stand,
And when you make it through
Reach back—
And help someone else do,
What we all know must be done,

Run Black Man run!
A fatherless child I may be,
But Mind, you belong to me
I decide who I choose to be!
Run Black Man Run
Run Black Man Run
Run Black Man Run!

In this poem, 'Twon makes the decision to replace negative thoughts with empowering ones. He makes the decision to transform his pain to power. He makes the decision to take control of his mind and define his own destiny. And so can you.

Through the power of the Authentic Self we can observe what we are thinking. And when those thoughts are negative, we must simply breathe, observe those thoughts, and from the Authentic Self feed ourselves new, empowering thoughts. It is important to remember the crucial steps of breath, then observation. These steps bring you into presence with your Authentic Self—the unlimited potential to create, do, or be anything.

Truly as a man thinks so is he.

Again, it is hard to *not do* something. It is easier and more effective to *do*. It is hard to tell yourself to stop thinking a thought. It is easier to replace that negative thought with a positive one. For example, it is hard to tell yourself, "Stop feeling insecure." It is more empowering to say, "I am a wonderful person, with many incredible qualities and I am actively working on becoming the best me I can be." Thoughts become things. Thoughts impact our emotions in a profound way. Truly as a man thinks so is he. Make the choice to take control of your thoughts and define your own destiny through the power of your Authentic Self.

REDEFINING ADDICTION THROUGH THE LENS OF THOUGHT

As I've shared earlier in the book, I grew up in a household where I was deeply impacted by addiction—both my father's addiction to heroin and my older brother's addiction to crack cocaine. I love both of these men very much, and it was painful and terrifying to see the impact their addiction was having firstly on them and then on the family as a whole.

Also, as child, I was terrified that I would grow up to be like my father and big brother and face the same challenges they were facing. After all, I looked like them. I thought it inevitable that I'd grow up to be like them. In response to this fear as a child, I immersed myself in my academics and hard work. Eventually, I would discover that a connection with my Authentic Self enabled me to embrace my power to define my own destiny rather than a fear that I was destined to be like my father and brother.

Too many of us have loved ones who suffer with addiction, perhaps a mother, father, sister, or brother. And many of us have our own addictive behavior with which we wrestle. I would like to empower you to expand your concept of how you define addiction. I am intentionally redefining the word in alignment with the concepts and tools I am sharing in this book.

> ADDICTION is the state of so identifying with your negative thoughts that you are at the mercy of those thoughts, and thereby incapable of accessing your power to create your life through your Authentic Self by making healthy, empowering choices.

When we define addiction in this manner, we discover that we all have addictive behavior. That addictive behavior is different for each of us. Have you ever had an extremely challenging day at work and so you manage it by overeating? Perhaps some of us have had a very challenging argument with someone we care deeply about, and we respond by going out and drinking with friends to the point of getting drunk. In both of these examples, the addictive behavior may not be so extreme that it is an everyday occurrence, but it is still an example of so identifying with negative thoughts that we disconnect from our Authentic Self and fail to make healthy, empowering choices. The level of addiction is just more extreme in people whose lives have reached the point of overwhelming dysfunction. One of the roots of addiction is a negative thought pattern that has become more pervasive than a person's connection with the Authentic Self—so pervasive that the person cannot access his or her Authentic Self and is thereby rendered incapable of making healthy, empowering choices.

Consider this comedic poem from my play *Through the Night*. In this poem an overweight bishop fights his addiction to food.

Angel Versus the Demon

I had a dream last night,
And all day long, my soul it ain't been right . . .
You see, there's a battle raging on the right and left side
    of me
An *Angel* and a **Demon** who won't let me be:
Now the Angel, she says: *Step away from the plate, go*
    exercise,
You can't just eat what you want and get the weight off those
    thighs.
There are more options than food when life gets you down,
Face it my brother you are three hundred pounds—
But then the Demon, she says: **Baby, forget that mess!**
Life is hard—eat what you want—manage the stress.
Big and sexy is in—who wants to be thin?
Getting tossed and torn with every blow of the wind.
Your fat keeps you standing, no matter what comes
    your way—
That's right, Big Man, you've got what it takes to stay.
But in what condition—out of breath—on the verge of death?
Knees giving in from the weight of all that heft—

There is more going on than a big appetite,
There are things going wrong, you just can't make right—
Girl, he just hungry—
So you eat more and more to make the pain disappear,
Sacrificing your health instead of facing your fear—
So you face it and then what? Pain doesn't go away—
You want to see more problems? Live another day.
Baby, we all find our ways to cope—you ain't smoking dope,
Pick up them chicken wings, have a 2-liter coke!
Angel and Demon will you leave me alone!
You're making me weak—I'm the Bishop I'm supposed to be strong!
Strong for everyone else and killing yourself—
We're all going to die sometime; go on and eat, it ain't a crime.
It's hard for me to hear with you both in my ear.
Then Demon be gone! Banished to the pits of Hell.
Come on now, Angel, you call that a spell?!
Yes—I demand you to go, leave, I insist!
What you doing, girl? This ain't The Exorcist!
Stop it! Please! Quit! You're making me sick!
Go on now, Demon, don't make me get cross.
Whatever, Angel, I'm only leaving 'cause God's your boss.
Big Man, come down and see me sometime.
Thank Heavens!

Now, Bishop, there will always be moments you feel out of
   control,
But it's in the midst of chaos you find the truth of your Soul:
Unlimited, Powerful, Resilient, Divine,
Godlike in nature if you can just find,
The Breath to reach past your fear,
Deep inside to the place where you hear:
Let go, surrender, the truth is you are held,
Carried on the wings of Angels, designed to quell,
Every worry, every fear, the truth is we are here.
The question:
Will I listen?
Hey, Big Man, you feeling hungry?

If we're honest, we'll admit we've all been engaged in this
battle in one form or another—wrestling in our own minds with
opposing thoughts. Unlike the character 'Twon in the previous
poem, "Run Black Man Run," the Bishop is completely lost in
the maze of his own thoughts. He's lost his ability to choose. He
is disconnected from his Authentic Self. He is in an addictive
state. Even though some of his thoughts are positive (not all
thoughts that come from an out-of-control mind are negative),
the Bishop still does not have true power in his life because he is
not in control of his mind.

Can you relate to this experience—wrestling in your own
mind with opposing thoughts when, in the depths of you, you
know what is right for you? I firmly believe that a first and cru-

cial step in addressing the addictive behaviors we all possess in one form or another is to simply breathe, observe our thoughts, and choose to replace those negative thoughts that feed our addictions with empowering thoughts that enable us to create the lives of our dreams. Certainly this is just one step in the complex journey to break addictive behavior, but it is a vital first step. We will discuss other steps in future chapters.

A POSITIVE MENTAL INHERITANCE

Sometimes your Mental Inheritance can be empowering, and it can inspire a legacy that impacts generations to come. Consider the words of John Lee, a Chinese-American from my play *Mr. Joy*. His father, a Chinese immigrant affectionately called Mr. Joy by his community, has run a shoe shop in Harlem for twenty-five years. In this poem, John Lee discovers his Mental Inheritance from his father.

Inheritance

My father has the same outfit he's worn for years—
Black shoes, gray pants, white shirt, black apron—
He has three sets, and wears them in rotation every week at
*   his shoe shop.*
I've offered countless times to take him on a shopping spree,
*   but he won't hear of it.*

He has given me the best education money can buy by shining
   shoes.
Chinese people—we take a little and make a lot.
One man's sacrifice can create possibility for his entire
   line . . .
That's my Inheritance—my father's sacrifice,
His work ethic, his discipline, his love—
My father—he's a simple man,
Doesn't have any fancy degrees,
But all of mine I owe to him,
And what he has taught me with his life
Is more priceless than the Ivy League education he
   afforded me—
How can I repay the gift of his integrity, his consistency, his
   love?
It's impossible, the best I can do is spend my Inheritance
   wisely,
And pass it on to my children—

EXERCISE:

Understanding Your Mental Inheritance

As stated earlier, your Mental Inheritance consists of the primary thought patterns you inherit/learn as a child from your primary caregiver(s) and your core community, through both conscious and unconscious suggestion. One way to clarify Mental Inheritance is to reflect on those common expressions parents often use when describing their children's behavior: "Oh, you got that from me," or "You're acting just like your mother/father."

Please take out your notebook and answer the following questions:

1. What patterns of thinking did you observe during your formative years from your primary caregivers? For example, did your mother always assume the worst would happen? Did your father say things like "We can't afford that," "We'll never be able to afford that"?

2. What ways of negotiating difficult situations, moving through the world, did you inherit in your formative years from your core community? Did you see a relative or friend not attempt his or her dreams out of fear? Did you see people retreat into themselves and become distant in the face of hard times rather than reach out to one another, or did you see people bond together and support one another when times were tough?

3. Now make a distinction for yourself between what aspects of your Mental Inheritance empower you and what aspects of your Mental Inheritance limit you.

4. Can you identify the impact your Mental Inheritance has had on your life? Through the power of your Authentic Self you can choose to use the aspects of your Mental Inheritance

that empower you and discard what limits you. It begins with awareness and the moment-to-moment decision to choose differently.

STATEMENTS OF AFFIRMATION

+ I have thoughts, but I am not my thoughts.

+ The Authentic Self is the parent to my thoughts.

+ And through my Authentic Self I can train my thoughts to empower me rather than limit me.

+ I must simply Breathe and Observe what I am thinking.

+ When a thought does not empower me, I must simply choose a new thought.

+ I have the power to choose the aspects of my Mental Inheritance that empower me and discard what disempowers me.

+ The very choice to Breathe and Observe leads to immediate presence with my Authentic Self—the unlimited potential to create, do, or be anything.

+ I understand that becoming present with my Authentic Self is a process.

+ I choose the process of conscious thought over being an unconscious victim of pervasive negative thinking.

✦ I am proclaiming my ability to transform my pain to power.

✦ I breathe and I boldly proclaim:

- *I am powerful!*

- *I am greater than my past!*

- *I am greater than any negative thoughts or feelings!*

- *I choose to be gentle, patient, and loving with myself.*

- *I am worthy of peace and joy.*

- *I am worthy of my dreams.*

4

The Power of Your Emotions and Your Emotional Inheritance

Dance Mama Dance

Mama . . . I saw you raise five of us by
yourself with a father nowhere in sight.
I saw you inspire revolution with a chicken and two potatoes.
I saw you limp home late at night after
a long day's work with sores on your feet.
I saw you gracefully remove groceries from
the cart when the bill got too high.
I saw you pray when brother stole the microwave to buy drugs.
I saw you make Christmas a ceremony and
I could've sworn we were royalty.
I saw you hold our home together like a foundation
that would never crumble.
But Mama, I never saw you dance. I never saw you dance.

And I wonder what happened to your music
'Cause I've got an instinct you still know how to groove,
So like a soulful incantation I write this dream for you:
I see you stand in a celestial ballroom lit by the moon.
I see you wear a gown of rose petals woven with gold thread.
I see you sparkle like the necklace of stars upon your neck.
I see you comfortable in shoes cut from the clouds.
I see you happy with a mate adoring every inch of your
essence—
And Mama, he looks like Denzel.
I see you laugh as Nina and Luther sing eternally for you
And Mama I see you dance. Yes, Mama I see you dance.
And I say Dance Mama Dance
Break the floodgates of countless uncried tears
And Dance Mama Dance
For all the nights you slept alone with no warm arms
to hold you
Dance Mama Dance
For all the dreams that you forgot so we could make it through
the day
Dance Mama Dance
Like your nightmare is ending
Like joy is beginning
Like life is not through with you yet
Laugh, Cry, Swirl, Twirl,
Dance Mama—Dance, Dance, Dance
Dance Mama—Dance!

My mother fought like hell through a racist South of the 1960s, through relationships where she was physically and emotionally abused, even through having one of her children taken from her by her mate as she attempted to escape to safety. My own father abandoned us to his heroin addiction and incarceration. In the midst of all this and more, she stands as one of the strongest, most loving, powerful human beings I have ever encountered. She has raised me and loved me through moments of personal insecurity, self-discovery, and doubt. Today I am proud to say I am a black man raised by a dynamic black woman.

She also passed on to me aspects of an EMOTIONAL INHERITANCE rooted in her unhealed wounds. My intention in sharing this is not to cast blame on my mother, though as a young person I did. Unfortunately, in a single parent home, the parent who was present too often gets the brunt of the attack when a child is in pain and endeavors to heal as an adult. But the truth is that parent was there and did her or his best to provide without the support of the partner who helped to create the child. Still, mistakes were inevitably made, and pretending that they did not happen does not help anyone. Neither does continuing to live in the pain of past hurts. However, an honest exploration of moments of breakdown can be healing for child and parent alike. Explorations of such moments were crucial for my personal healing as well as for healing my relationship with my mother. My mother has healed through the years, and her transformation has been remarkable, but it is still important for me to share this core aspect of my Healing Journey, with the intention of encouraging the possibility of healing in others.

> Your EMOTIONAL INHERTANCE is the primary emotional landscape you inherit/learn from your primary caregiver(s) and core community as a child through both conscious and unconscious suggestion.

There was an Emotional Inheritance of sadness, pain, and low self-esteem, and a resulting behavior pattern of being a workaholic that I inherited from my mother. The words that are spoken to us as children by our principal caregiver(s) can have a resounding impact on how we process our own emotions. Also, the predominant emotions we see our parents embody can greatly impact how we develop our inner emotional landscape.

For much of my life I felt unattractive. My skin is darker in complexion than that of the other members of my family, and my mother would often make comments like "Stay out of the sun, you don't want to get any darker" or "You're too dark to wear those bright colors. Take off that red!"

When I was in high school, she gave me a jar of a skin product called Nadinola—a product defined by the manufacturer as "a skin discoloration fade cream." As an adult I now understand this product is designed to even your skin tone. This product can also lighten your complexion. As a child and into my early adulthood, I was absolutely convinced my mother hated my dark skin and thought I was ugly. My nose is also wider than the noses of the other members of my family, and my mother would even occasionally rub the sides of my nose, pulling it toward the center, as if attempting to magically make it more pointed and less wide. Once when she returned home from a vacation, my gift was a mug with a very unattractive man on it, and it read, "God gave me the choice between money and good looks. I chose money."

On the upside of my Healing Journey, these comments and experiences are comical to me, but as a child and into my early adulthood, they were deeply painful. Fortunately, some "Angels" appeared in my life that replaced my negative Emotional Inheritance with a positive one and aided my healing.

Part of my training is as an opera singer. While studying at Yale, the renowned African-American opera diva Leontyne Price performed a concert. I had the pleasure of spending some time with her after she sang. The first words she said to me were, "Your skin is beautiful like ebony alabaster." I was stunned when she spoke these words to me because at that point I had never even considered that my dark skin was beautiful. The experience of her elegance and her emotional embrace impacted me deeply. As I departed the room, I turned to get one last glance at this remarkable woman. She was looking in my direction, and once again she mouthed the words "ebony alabaster."

Another healing moment transpired when I had the opportunity to spend time with the internationally renowned African-American theater director and producer Ellen Stewart at her villa and artist retreat in Spoleto, Italy. Ellen Stewart, who passed in 2011, was the founder of La Mama Experimental Theatre Club in New York City. She was affectionately called "Mama" by her "children" across the globe. I was performing a series of concerts throughout Italy over the summer of 1997, and during a week's vacation, I had the opportunity to sit by her side. One night I was sharing with her some of my insecurities about my appearance, and the power of her response still resonates in the depths of my soul to this day. She said to me, "Let me tell you how beautiful you are, my child. Your features are distinctly African in nature, and I have traveled the globe, and some of the most beautiful statues in the world carved from the most valuable stone are crafted to look just like you. Never doubt how beautiful you are."

These two phenomenal women provided me with a new perspective to combat the negative Emotional Inheritance I had received from my mother. These experiences, combined with years of affirmations as I described in Chapter One, have completely shifted my self-concept. Today, I embrace the sun and understand that bright colors actually highlight my dark complexion. And I can appreciate the value of a smooth, even skin tone, especially for someone who is constantly in the public eye. But as a child, it was a very different story.

When I confronted my mother about the negative impact her words and actions had on me as a child, she was shocked, and she assured me that she didn't think I was unattractive. But further investigation into her own story caused me to discover that my mother was unconsciously transmitting to me her own negative emotional self-concept. The following is a brief excerpt of a letter my mother wrote to me during my Healing Journey, after I had challenged her to be real about some of the pain she had passed on to me.

> *I was a daddy's girl, and when I was nine or ten my daddy left us and started another family. I became insecure about my own attractiveness and self-worth. I tried to replace my daddy's love with all kinds of men including your father, and got myself involved in so much drama I should be dead. It was only when I began to get real with myself that I discovered I had deep wounds only God could heal.*

My mother is an astonishingly beautiful woman inside and out. And for much of her life she did not fully believe in or own her beauty because of her Initial Breakdown with her father's abandonment. I found one of my mother's yearbooks from high school. She was the homecoming queen, but she cut her face out of the picture because she did not like the way she looked. My mother's first marriage was to a man who physically abused her. This destructive relationship was followed by her relationship with my father, and I have already shared with you many details about how that story unfolded. It makes sense that my mother would pass some of her unhealed pain on to her children.

Why not *choose* to feel good?

My mother also provided. This too is part of my Emotional Inheritance from my mother. She was consistent and she was there. She modeled tenacity and determination by her persistence. Our house was filled with self-help books she had no time to read because she was working until ten o'clock at night. As I shared in my poem "Dance Mama Dance," she always made Christmas a ceremony, as if trying to pour into that single day all the love she did not have the time, energy, or money to express throughout the year. And in the past decade she has made her emotional healing a priority.

YOU ARE NOT YOUR FEELINGS

Do you have emotions or do your emotions have you? You have feelings, but you are not your feelings. Negative thoughts create negative feelings. When you are experiencing negative feelings, simply breathe, observe what you are thinking, and choose to feed yourself thoughts that make you feel good.

Try it now. Take three cleansing breaths in through your nose and out through your mouth. Observe what you are thinking *and* feeling in this moment. Now feed yourself these thoughts:

I am attractive!

Every inch of my skin is beautiful!

I am intelligent!

I am a good person!

I am loving and I am loved!

I am amazing and life is amazing!

I am powerful beyond belief!

Now how do you feel? I am not suggesting that we become emotional robots who never feel sadness or anger or the vast range of human emotions. But we spend way too much time feeling poorly, and often those feelings have nothing to do with the present moment. Often those feelings are rooted in past pain or future anxiety. Times when you can choose to be sad or angry or any of the vast range of human emotions will appear without your dwelling on past pain or worrying about the future. People die, relationships end, jobs are lost, close friends move away—things happen. But each breath is a moment when you can *choose* to feel good. Why not *choose* to feel good?

THE POWER OF SORROW

There are times in our lives when our emotions are so intense and the situation so traumatic that we must give them space, and failure to do so can have profound consequences. Remember: that which we resist persists. For example, when someone we love dies we must give ourselves time to grieve. I was at work when I learned of my grandmother's death. I thought I was fine and continued working. Before I realized what was happening, I was in a pool of tears in front of my coworkers. My grief was demanding space.

Likewise, when a deeply buried wound is unearthed, we must allow ourselves space to feel the emotion connected with that wound before we can forgive, heal, and move on. Otherwise, we are just placing a bandage on a festering sore.

For as long as I could remember, I had a subtle image that would appear in my dreams and sometimes in my waking moments. The image was of myself as a child in the shower with a shadowy figure who looked like a man. The vision was so subtle that it would appear quickly in my mind's eye and then vanish. Often when people would recount stories of their childhoods, they would have such vivid memories and details. So many of my memories of my childhood were absent. To this day I can look at pictures of myself as a child and have no recollection of when and where the picture was taken.

During the end of my senior year in high school, I attended a church retreat where I had the opportunity as a youth leader to support hundreds of young people through their Healing Journey. As I was praying with one young man, I heard a quiet voice in my head say, "As you help others to heal, I am healing you." This subtle vision I had had for as long as I could remember became more persistent throughout the retreat. I could not ignore it, but I did not understand what it was.

When I returned home, I kneeled beside my bed to pray. As I closed my eyes and began to pray, the entire vision of my molestation as a child by an older male figure in my family played vividly through my mind. I had repressed the experience so deeply that previous to this moment I had not remembered it, or most of the rest of my childhood for that matter, except for the subtle image that I mentioned previously. I immediately began weeping, and my body convulsed with the depth of the pain I was experiencing. I tried to resist the painful memory that was flooding my mind and my heart. I looked around my room at the trophies and plaques I had received throughout my childhood—my badges of triumph and success—crying, "This image of this little boy being violated—that's not me. These awards, these symbols of achievement—these are me." This was a moment when my Resulting Behavior Pattern, "I will achieve to the point of exhaustion to prove to myself and others that I am worthy to be loved," was not—could not—be greater than my past pain.

My mother heard me screaming and rushed up the stairs. After I recounted the story of what I had discovered, she prayed with me and then we watched a videotape of a T. D. Jakes sermon about forgiveness. Within an hour of this devastating discovery, I was professing forgiveness for the man who had molested me as a child. I mean, I was a youth leader, a Christian, on my way to Yale and an amazing life, this was what I was supposed to do, right? I was supposed to forgive.

Well, about two months later, during my freshman year at Yale, as I worked in the library (I worked five days a week as an undergraduate to help pay my tuition), I was reading a magazine that featured a letter to Oprah written by a little girl who had been molested. Oprah had previously announced the upcoming release of an autobiography in which she was going to express how she had forgiven those who had molested her. The little girl, having been molested herself, asked Oprah how she could possibly forgive the people who had done this to her. The article suggested that as a result of that letter, Oprah had subsequently chosen not to release that book. I have not yet met Oprah, though it is one of my dreams to know this phenomenal human being. I do not know if the sequence of events reported in this article is true. But in the moment of reading these words, sitting in that library at Yale, a well of pain emerged that mirrored what I had experienced that day when the vision of my molestation first surfaced for me. I completely broke down at the desk, had to leave my job, wept and convulsed all the way to my dorm room, and lay in my bed for several days to allow the space this trauma required.

There is a time for sorrow. Sometimes the depth of pain is so deep you must give it the space it requires in order to heal, forgive, and move on. Today, I have forgiven, but it was certainly a process—a process that we will discuss in a future chapter.

THE POWER OF ANGER

Just as there are times when we must allow ourselves to grieve and feel sorrow, there are times when we must allow ourselves to feel anger. Many people who are sad and depressed—even numb—actually have deep-seated anger, sometimes rage, that they have never expressed. As a result, they've turned that anger inward. If your dominant negative feeling is sorrow, perhaps there is a reservoir of repressed rage in you that needs expression. Sometimes we have to give space to our anger in order to move through it.

> Sometimes we have to give space to our anger in order to move through it.

The following poem is for anyone who has ever screamed a silent scream when it wasn't appropriate to scream out loud.

BANG!

Aw hell naw. He is not stopping me.

I don't have time for this, man.

Yes, Officer. Is there a problem?

Yes, this is my car—

ID? May I ask why? I mean, was I speeding—

Excuse me, sir, but there's no need to raise your voice.

Fine then. I'll get it—

No need for a gun—

My ID is in my left-hand pocket. I'm just getting it.

BANG! You don't know me.

Man, I live on this block, third house on the right.

Come over for dinner sometime, fried chicken and caviar.

*I've got a college degree, making a hundred thousand dollars
     a year*

*And you still want to stop me in my Beamer, thinking I'm a
     drug dealer.*

I don't have time for this, man. I'm over it.

*I'm seeking liberty at any cost and offering it to everybody
     who enters my realm.*

*That cop thought he was a bigoted authority figure who
     was going to ruin my day. BANG! I just freed his mind.*

*No more of this kumbaya my Lord, we shall overcome bull
     crap.*

Just BANG!

*So, when my Beamer's in the shop and a cabby passes me by
    on the street . . .*
*Hey, man, I'm already late! What, you think I won't tip?
    Here's one . . .*
BANG! You don't know me.
When a woman clenches her purse and crosses the street . . .
Actually, ma'am, Coach is not my brand. I prefer Hermès.
BANG! You don't know me.
When the clerk follows me through the store at Macy's . . .
*What are you looking at? I can buy ten of these leather coats
    if I want them.*
BANG! You don't know me.
When my divinity is deemed dirty . . . BANG!
*When they call my anger "The Black Man's Disease" . . .
    BANG!*
*When they silence, deny, and reject my voice . . . BANG!
    BANG! BANG!*
AW HELL NAW!
Excuse me?
Oh yes, Officer, my ID . . . I'll get it.
My ID is in my left-hand pocket. I'll get it.
Here it is.
Where did my mind just go?
BANG!

REDEFINING ADDICTION THROUGH THE LENS OF EMOTION

In the previous chapter, we discovered that a negative Thought Pattern is one of the roots of addiction. Again I am consciously expanding our concept of addiction to empower us to use the tools I am sharing in this book.

I say again, ADDICTION is the state of so identifying with your negative thoughts that you are at the mercy of those thoughts, and thereby incapable of accessing your power through your Authentic Self to make healthy, empowering choices.

Another root of addiction is a negative Emotional Landscape. Often the addictive substance or behavior is abused in an effort to suppress the negative Emotional Landscape that has over-whelmed our access to the Authentic Self.

One of the keys to ending addictive behavior is to become present to this Emotional Landscape and begin the work of unpacking how you arrived at this place. That work is the focus of the concepts and exercises I am putting forth in this book: *Initial Breakdown, Resulting Thought Pattern, Dominating Emotional Landscape, Resulting Behavior Pattern, Authentic Self, Mental and Emotional Inheritance, and so forth.*

If you do the work, you will know the truth of who you are.

Then day by day, sometimes moment by moment, you must *choose* to live in that truth—the truth of your Authentic Self.

Another key to breaking addiction is to truly become present to the emotional impact your addiction is having not only on you as an individual, but on the people you love. How does my addictive behavior impact my mate, my children? Does it make them afraid of me or for me? Does it cause them to view me as inconsistent with my word and my commitments? Do I make promises that I do not keep? Does my addictive behavior keep me from making positive contributions to their lives or modeling positivity by creating the life of my dreams? How do I truly feel about myself? How do I truly feel about the way my behavior, my choices, my addiction have impacted those I love? This process is about using emotion to create a positive outcome rather than allowing negative emotions to overwhelm you to the point of destruction. Once we are truly aware of the negative impact of our addictive behavior on others, we have fuel that we can reference in the moment of choice. That fuel is love. I'm not suggesting the process is easy, but when we can truly understand and feel how our behavior is hurting people we love dearly, we can make the choice to remember the negative impact of our behavior at the moment of choice. There are many other support networks, like Alcoholics Anonymous and the various other 12-step groups, that offer powerful, multilayered support networks for managing addiction. I am not suggesting that this one tool will be a cure-all. I am merely offering another valuable tool to add to the toolbox. Again, I am speaking of recovery technology—tools that operate at the pace of our modern lives. When picking up that drink, there is space when one can choose love. How will this choice, in this moment, impact me and those I love? When we become truly present to the emotional impact of our destructive, addictive behavior, on oursleves and others, we will be less likely to engage in it.

The following passage is a continuation of the "Angel Versus the Demon" poem from the previous chapter. Ellen is the Bishop's wife. Remember, the Bishop is battling a food addiction. His particular vice is HoHos—the round chocolate cakes with cream in the center. Ellen's words illuminate both the root of addiction as well as the emotional impact it can have on those you love.

I hear him sneaking around at night with his chocolate delights.
But I pretend to be asleep to not embarrass him.
He's an addict and diabetes kills.
Addiction is the inability to value what is sacred—love is
    sacred,
And staying alive for love—for me, our son, our congregation—
Is less valuable to him than a HoHo—
HoHo—it's a funny word, but I'm not laughing.
He's a good man, he's my man, and my good man could die.
And I haven't loved all these years to grow old alone.
I want to love him when my hand shakes as I make his dinner
And his hand shakes as he lifts the fork—
Muscles weak from a lifetime of heavy living—
I want to love him when we place our teeth in a jar

And only eat soft foods—
Mouths tired from an overabundance of kisses.
I want to love him when our best moments are hard to remember
Our minds so full of living some fall out—
There's beauty in a love that lasts—
Not talking about young love or new love,
But long-lasting love—decades of knowing
He's a good man—he's my man,
And I don't need him skinny, but I need him alive.

EXERCISE:

Understanding Your Emotional Inheritance

Again, your Emotional Inheritance is the primary emotional landscape you inherit/learn from your primary caregiver(s) and core community as a child through both conscious and unconscious suggestion.

Please take out your notebook and answer the following questions:

1. What ways of emotionally responding to difficult situations do you remember witnessing from your primary caregivers growing up? Did your father become enraged easily when challenged? Did your mother sometimes go to her room and cry quietly rather than speak up for herself? Or perhaps your mother would go on bold tirades when angry and your father would emotionally shut down or match her anger?

2. What emotional landscape did you observe from your primary caregivers growing up? Were the people around you generally happy? Was the house full of laughter, music, dancing, hugs, and kisses? Or were the people around you often sad and angry, disconnected from one another? Did people support one another's success? Or were people jealous when one person did very well?

3. Now make a distinction for yourself between the aspects of your Emotional Inheritance that empower you and the aspects of your Emotional Inheritance that limit you. Can you identify the impact your Emotional Inheritance has had on your life? Through the power of your Authentic Self you can choose to use the aspects of your Emotional Inheritance that empower you and discard what limits you. It begins with awareness and the moment-to-moment decision to choose differently.

EXERCISE:

Write the Past/Create the Future

Using the model of my poem "Dance Mama Dance" at the beginning of this chapter, take out your notebook and complete the following steps:

1. Think of one of your primary caregivers growing up. Write the name as if you are speaking to him/her. For example, **"Mama . . ."**

2. Think about some of the tough times you made it through together. Someone died or went away. Someone got his/her heart broken. Money was short and times were hard. For example, when I think of my mother as I was growing up, I think of all the things she gave up, how hard she worked so that her children could be comfortable.

"I saw you limp home late at night after a long day's work with sores on your feet."

3. Use your memory of those experiences to **Write the Past**. Write at least five examples.

4. Think about how the future can be better. Dream big, be creative. **Create the Future.** Write at least five examples. Perhaps some of the examples in the future are in direct response to the examples from the past.

"I saw you limp home late at night after a long day's work with sores on your feet."

"I see you comfortable in shoes cut from the clouds."

a. *Find a chorus for your poem: two to five words that are the heart of your dream for the future. For example, "Dance Mama Dance!"*

b. *Find places in your poem to include the chorus.*

------

c. *Make it your own! Your personality! Your rhythms! Your style! This is your unique expression. Do this for yourself. Use the power of your emotion to transform your relationship to this past experience.*

The following are words to help you get started:

Write the Past	Create the Future
I saw . . .	*I see . . .*
You were . . .	*You are . . .*
I watched as you . . .	*I watch as you . . .*
I remember you . . .	*I imagine you . . .*

STATEMENTS OF AFFIRMATION

◆ I have thoughts and I have feelings, but I am not my thoughts and I am not my feelings.

◆ The Authentic Self is the parent to my thoughts and feelings.

◆ And through my Authentic Self I can train my thoughts and feelings to empower me rather than limit me.

◆ Thoughts create feelings.

◆ I must simply Breathe and Observe what I am thinking.

◆ When a thought does not empower me, I must simply choose a new thought.

✦ New, empowering thoughts will create new, empowering feelings.

✦ The very choice to Breathe and Observe leads to immediate presence with my Authentic Self—the unlimited potential to create, do, or be anything.

✦ I understand that becoming present with my Authentic Self is a process.

✦ I choose the process of conscious thought and feeling over being an unconscious victim of pervasive negative thinking and negative emotions.

✦ I am proclaiming my ability to transform my pain to power.

✦ I breathe and I boldly proclaim:

   • *I am powerful!*

   • *I am greater than my past!*

   • *I am greater than any negative thoughts or feelings!*

   • *I choose to be gentle, patient, and loving with myself.*

   • *I am worthy of peace and joy.*

   • *I am worthy of my dreams.*

5

The Power of Forgiveness and Letting Go

If you keep another person in the prison of your pain,
You have to stay to be the jailer.

After years of writing letters and visiting my father in prison, I began to understand the factors that led him to make such destructive choices. Part of my healing process was to write my father as a character so that I could journey the path of his thoughts and emotions. The following excerpt from my play *Trinity* is my father's true story, but it is written in my words.

> I guess the first thing I want you to know is that I'm sorry for the pain I've caused you.
>
> Being in prison all these years has given me time to reflect. I am not evil and that means you are not evil. There is nothing in your blood—nothing in your DNA. And I'm not stupid.

My IQ is 149. I never found anything I couldn't do. I made some bad choices and I'm a product of my environment.

I grew up in a small town in Virginia and there was a candy store in the neighborhood. I was about six or seven, and it was the late fifties. I was with my father. And my father was my hero, he was a man, you know what I'm saying. What he said was the law. To this day, the only man I was ever afraid of was my father.

I was a kid, I wanted some candy, knew my father didn't have no money to buy it, so I slipped some in my pocket. We are at the door about to walk out when the owner says, "Boy, that little nigger of yours stole from me." My father turns around and says, "Sir, what did you say? What did you call me? What did you call my son?" The owner says, "I said, boy, your little nigger stole from me. He got my candy in his pocket."

And I knew it was on, I knew my daddy was about to whip that cracker's ass. My father stared the owner straight in the eyes for about twenty seconds, then he looked at me and said, "Danny, empty your pockets." I had about three or four pieces of candy, maybe worth five cents. My father took the candy from me, then took out his wallet and placed a dollar on the counter. Then, he said, "Sir, I am very sorry." And we walked out.

I lost all respect for my daddy that day. At that point, there was no man I feared.

When I was seven or eight, in the 1950s, my dad uprooted our family from middle class Southern under my grandmother's money to dirt poor urban. I was only a child, but I knew the difference. My mother went to work as a housekeeper for a wealthy white family, and after school I would meet her at their home. The children were spoiled beyond belief. The family had everything and they were always happy. I hated being poor, and I resented not having immediate opportunity.

Across the street from us lived a gangster and his family had everything too. And they were black and they were happy. And I figured it out real quick: I would never be white, but I could be a gangster. I made up my mind at that early age what I wanted to be. Since then, whenever I thought about survival, wealth, money, I automatically thought, What illegal scheme can I do? *That was always my mind-set—never get a job, earn an honest living. Gangster. That's simply the way it was. I was arrested for the first time when I was ten years old for stealing valuable watches.*

Stepping inside my father's pain enabled me to forgive him. This monologue based on true events in my father's childhood clarifies my father's Initial Breakdown, the negative thoughts and emotions that emerged, and the Resulting Behavior Pattern.

Hurting people hurt people. My father wounded me because he was wounded himself. True compassion and understanding for the situation of the person who harmed you is a crucial step in forgiveness. How could I not forgive my father once I understood his pain? It was time for me to set us both free.

The reality is that he was not there. The unfortunate reality is that he continues to make destructive choices in terms of his addiction and his responsibility to himself and to those he loves. So I have had to set boundaries to keep myself safe. But I am no longer bound by feelings of guilt and resentment toward my father.

> True compassion and understanding for the situation of the person who harmed you is a crucial step in forgiveness.

Is there someone in your life that it has been challenging for you to forgive? In your heart, you may have even wanted to forgive this person, but for some reason there is still resentment. I would encourage you to try writing a first person monologue from that person's perspective. You can use the terms we've defined this far as a guide.

FORGIVING YOURSELF

Another core aspect of forgiveness is the choice to forgive one's self, and for many people this can be even more challenging than forgiving others. We all make mistakes. We all lash out because of our unhealed pain. Often we hurt the people closest to us the most. Whenever possible we must make amends with those we have harmed. In some instances this will not be possible because a person has passed or will refuse to be in communication.

Asking for forgiveness can be a challenging process because it means admitting to others that we have wronged them. It requires a level of soul-searching, humility, and vulnerability that can be daunting. We are also making ourselves vulnerable to others' anger, pain, and, potentially, refusal to forgive.

I offer a few valuable thoughts to help you negotiate this process. First, I find it is important to be very honest with yourself about the hurt that occurred and what role you played in it. You have to be crystal clear even if the other person is not ready or willing to admit their role in the situation, that this choice to ask for forgiveness is foremost a gift to yourself. You are restoring integrity and walking down the path to being the best, most loving person you can be.

Second, you must be very honest with yourself about the outcome you are hoping to achieve with your request for forgiveness, and be willing to be okay with the reality that you might not achieve that outcome. You must release control. You cannot use your request for forgiveness to manipulate an outcome. The request must be a pure gift to yourself and then to another. Yes, be honest with yourself about what you want, and honest with the other person about what you want, but do not let that be the reason for the request. Do you want to restore a relationship? That may or may not happen. When we are okay with this reality, we are truly ready to ask forgiveness, while at the same time taking care of ourselves.

Third, you must be willing to make a commitment, first to yourself and then to that person, about how your behavior will change. Often you will need to allow time to regain trust and for that person to see if you will keep your commitment. A hurt has happened, and sometimes words are not enough to restore a relationship. Often one must take consistent new action.

Last, you must try to forgive yourself. We all make mistakes. Frequently, mistakes are the results of our pain that we haven't quite figured out how to heal. We must forgive ourselves not as an excuse but as a crucial step on the path to our healing and becoming the best people we possibly can. If the person we hurt will not forgive us, we must still learn to forgive ourselves.

Oftentimes we have hurt ourselves by not protecting our minds, bodies, hearts, or spirits. Personally, I felt a great deal of anger toward myself for years for not being able to feel better, to be happier, to just get over the pain. I remember thinking, *Daniel, you have all these amazing things happening in your life, why can't you just get over the past, get over your pity party, and be grateful?* I tried time and time again to guilt myself into feeling better. But the truth we have already discovered is that negative thoughts and feelings (such as guilt) only create more negativity. I was only able to begin to heal when I chose to be gentler with myself, to acknowledge that I had done the best I could—and sometimes I hadn't, and that was okay too.

We all make mistakes. Sometimes we know better and we still don't make the right choices. This is part of being human. The question becomes, how can we increase the possibility of making choices that empower us and other people? Forgiving one's self, being gentle with one's self, and building from a place of positive thoughts and feelings will always get us farther than blaming ourselves and tearing ourselves down.

Say, for example, a person has an issue with overeating. She makes a commitment to a specific eating and exercise plan. She is having a terribly difficult time with an overbearing boss at work. Perhaps her children are also misbehaving, and she has an argument with her husband about taking more responsibility in rearing the children. Frustrated, she skips the gym and instead calls a friend to complain about her husband and kids. At lunch she overeats to manage her stress. Rather than stopping there, she thinks, *Well, I already messed up.* She starts to feed herself negative thoughts: *I don't have the support I need. I hate this job. My husband is so selfish. I already messed up today so I might as well keep going.* She goes to the break room and there is leftover birthday cake, and she has a slice or two. She continues like this all the way through to a midnight snack, and this may continue for days, even weeks. At any point in this process, she could have stopped and made a new choice. Even after skipping the gym, she could have made better food choices. Instead of complaining to her friend, she could have asked for support in thinking through her thoughts and feelings. She could have requested support in keeping her commitments to herself. And once she broke her integrity to herself, she could have stopped, evaluated what had occurred, forgiven herself, and made a new commitment.

Again, we all make mistakes often. Frequently, those mistakes are triggered by past or current pain or feeling overwhelmed. At any point, we can stop, observe what we are thinking and feeling, and make a new choice. When this is challenging for us, we can ask friends and loved ones for support in making healthy choices, rather than keeping it to ourselves or only speaking to those who will support our complaints or pity parties. And when we make mistakes, which we inevitably will, we can be honest about what happened, forgive ourselves, make new commitments, and try again.

> ## As you forgive others, give that same forgiveness to yourself.

What mistakes have you still not forgiven yourself for? Have you done everything you can to make amends with the person you have harmed? What will it take for you to finally forgive yourself and let it go? Now is the time. As you forgive others, give that same forgiveness to yourself.

THE POWER OF LETTING GO

It is a reality of life that painful and disappointing experiences have occurred and will continue to occur in our lives. We must know when to let that pain and disappointment go rather than holding on to it and allowing it to turn into bitterness and frustration. Maybe your plan didn't work out because that which you desired was smaller than your ultimate purpose. Maybe it is time to embrace a bigger vision than your immediate disappointment.

Once you have allowed yourself sufficient time to experience the emotion of the pain you have experienced, there is power in choosing to let it go. But I don't subscribe to the "forgive and forget" philosophy. My view is "forgive and transform—transform that pain to power."

We will talk more about this process in future chapters, but right now I invite you to ponder the following questions: What has the experience of this pain taught you? How has this pain strengthened you and made you an overcomer? What have you learned from the experience of this pain that could be useful to someone else? There is both power and possibility in our pain when we choose to let it go and allow it to transform.

DON'T ALLOW A SEASON TO BECOME A LIFETIME

Loss of a loved one, loss of a job, loss of a relationship—there is a proper time of mourning, but we cannot allow a season of mourning to turn into a lifetime of sorrow. When you have been wronged, there is a proper time for anger. But you cannot move swiftly into your future with the baggage of past disappointments weighing you down. Why did I have this miscarriage? Why did this person leave me? Why was I born into this family? There are some answers we will never know. At some point we must make up our minds and hearts that we are not going to spend our lives trying to figure out things we cannot possibly know. Some things just don't make sense, and we have to be tenacious about ushering in a new season of healing and empowerment for our lives.

The following comedic monologue from my musical *Tearing Down the Walls* reveals one woman's struggle to release the anger that has permeated her life. The speaker is named Rhonda.

BEAUTY VERSUS THE BEAST

There's a battle going on inside of me,
Between my rough exterior and the softness I used to be.
It's a battle you see between the Beauty and the Beast in me.
Now, the Beauty she says,
Darling, comb your hair. Your weave is nappy!
Sure life can be crappy, but that's no excuse for self-abuse.
But then the Beast she says,
Shut up, Beauty, it's my duty to be crass—
When a man hurts me, I KICK HIS ASS!
And your weave is sweated out and you're sad and alone,
At home on a Friday night sitting by the phone,
Homely, horny, and hopeless,
Yes, Beast, you can quote this:
When you look that rough, it gone be tough to get a man.
Why get a man just to give him back?
So many of these brothers out here are whack,

Talking about baby I'm going to love you till the end,
Then you turn your back and they're getting in
With your best friend and so then I KICK HIS ASS!
You are a hopeless case—what a waste!
You could be so much more with just a little taste.
You keep it up, you gone taste my foot in yo' as—
As I was saying, there are other ways to be than angry.
Softness has a power you cannot always see—
A gentle love of self despite the pain you have faced,
A power that only emanates from confidence and grace—
But I've been hurt before and I ain't gettin' hurt no
more.
But you're just pouring salt on a sore,
You're letting them win time and time again.
First they hurt you and now you're hurting you too—
Child, you are hard on the eyes,
And I surmise, when you look in the mirror you don't like
what you see—
But deep inside you there is still a Beauty,
Beast, free me from this cage of rage,
And you won't have to go it alone.
Outside you can be beautiful and inside still be strong.
Try this for a while and I promise you will see the power of
your own Beauty
Please, Beast, will you set me free?
I guess we can try, but if he cheats on me,
I'm still going to KICK HIS ASS!

In this poem, Rhonda has been disappointed and bruised so many times by dysfunctional relationships with men that she cannot even consider the possibility of a healthy, loving one. Moreover, she has allowed her disappointment to transform into bitterness so much so that it impacts her appearance and self-care. And to top it all off, she's been abused so often that she embodies the persona of the abuser by beating men up when they cheat on her. This character is purposely extreme to illustrate a point. But how extreme is Rhonda's behavior, truly? Think of people you see walking down the street, on your job, perhaps even when you look in the mirror. Often you can see the stories of their pain on their faces, and sometimes it impacts their self-care. And we all know people—some of us are or have been those people—who have experienced so much pain that they assume the stance that they will hurt first before they will allow themselves to be hurt. This behavior does not have to be as extreme as Rhonda's. It can manifest as being overly defensive, being quick to anger, being emotionally distant to the point of being antisocial, and a myriad of other negative behaviors. If we are not careful, we can build a wall between others and ourselves.

Tearing Down the Walls

Don't know how to tear down the walls
Been building so long done built me in
And it's safe, a little cold, but safe
And I can afford the rent

Cheaper than that love shit
And last time I was homeless
I vowed never again
Would I pay that kinda fee
So I'm living with me
Visitor now and then
Maybe a friend
No sublets, no tenants
Definitely no lease
I own it
And it' safe, a little cold, but safe—
Been building so long done built me in.
Don't know how to tear down the walls.

KEEP YOUR PAST IN THE PAST AND NOT IN YOUR PRESENT OR YOUR FUTURE

Past experiences are simply thoughts and emotions crafted into vivid stories—stories so vivid that we believe they define us, that these stories are who we are. If we identify this fully with our past, our present and future are already full and there is no space for a new possibility to emerge. In other words we believe, "It happened like this in the past, so it will probably happen like this in the future," and that closes off any opportunity for us. For example, if we enter a new romantic relationship believing that our new partner will be the same or even similar to the previous one, we do not create sufficient space for a new, powerful relationship to emerge. We will evaluate that new partner's behavior based on past experiences. We may even place expectations on that new partner based on how the previous one behaved. We can absolutely convince ourselves that we have people—men or women—figured out, when the reality is that every single individual is unique. And if you look for proof that you are right or that your assumptions are correct, you will inevitably find it. You may even unknowingly create the proof you need. Let's say, for instance, that you had a previous partner who was quick to anger. You have a fear, perhaps even an expectation, that your new partner will be the same. So you identify his/her triggers and push buttons to confirm your suspicions, your fears. And, of course, you end up being right!

A better option would be honesty with yourself (and your new partner when the time is right) about your past pain and fear, and then imagining, creating, and staying committed to the vision of what you truly desire for yourself in a romantic relationship. You must then be vigilant about examining the thoughts and feelings that have kept you separate from your deepest desires in the past, and you must stay committed to the new thoughts and feelings that will empower you to create the relationship you truly want. This process will allow you to be in this new relationship from a space of creativity and possibility instead of one of fear and past pain. You may worry, "What if this person hurts me or I miss the signs of negative behavior because I don't have my guard up?" The process I am suggesting will allow you to be even more present to that individual, and you will even be more likely to know when something is off if you're not looking for it or expecting it.

Sometimes the pain is so deeply rooted, we're not even aware of the patterns we are repeating or the negativity we are anticipating will appear in our lives. If you truly desire a particular outcome, like a beautiful, affirming romantic relationship, and continue to produce the opposite, there is a strong possibility that there are deep-seated patterns of which you are unaware. One goal of this book is to help you understand those patterns.

The following exercise is designed to empower you to release your past pain once and for all so that you can take ownership of your story in a manner that empowers you rather than limits you. This exercise is designed to take your past out of your future so that you can have an open space to create the life of your dreams.

EXERCISE:
Your Life Story

1. Set an alarm clock for thirty minutes. Now write the story of your pain. Write every painful experience you can think of that has happened up to this point in your life. Allow your thoughts to flow and do not censor yourself. In particular, focus on the "big" moments in your life that you feel are crucial to how you identify in the world. These "big" moments are the ones you would only share with those most intimate

with you. Allow yourself the biggest pity party you can imagine. Indulge. Let it out once and for all.

2. Find a mirror and read your life story over and over to yourself until the story no longer has an emotional charge for you. Read this story over and over again to yourself to the point of tedium. If it takes an hour, do it.

If you commit fully to this exercise, you will discover that your life story is just that, a story. You possess your story—it does not possess you. You are not defined by it. And like any story, if you keep telling it over and over, it becomes predictable, tedious, and boring. When will you become fed up enough with your own painful story that you will commit to creating a new one? You have past painful experiences, but you have the power through your presence with your Authentic Self to choose not to be defined or limited by those experiences.

STATEMENTS OF AFFIRMATION

✦ Through the power of Breath and Observation I access my Authentic Self—the unlimited power to create, do, or be *anything*.

✦ My Authentic Self is the parent to my thoughts and feelings.

✦ I have thoughts and I have feelings, but I am not my thoughts and I am not my feelings.

✦ When I have negative thoughts and feelings, I must simply Observe what I am thinking and feeling and through presence with my Authentic Self choose new, empowering thoughts and feelings.

✦ Sometimes this is a moment-by-moment process, but I choose conscious thoughts and feelings over being a victim to pervasive negative thoughts and feelings.

✦ I have some painful past experiences, but I choose not to be limited by those experiences.

✦ I choose to forgive myself and other people.

✦ I will not allow a season of sorrow and anger to become a lifetime.

✦ I have agency and power in my life.

✦ I am proclaiming my ability to transform my pain to power.

✦ I understand that in the process of my healing, some negative, painful experiences and memories will emerge.

✦ I allow the space for my thoughts and feelings, even though they may be painful, because I know that my intention is to create the life of my dreams.

✦ Even though I may not think or feel it in this moment, I boldly proclaim:

- *I am powerful!*

- *I am greater than my past!*

- *I am greater than any negative thoughts or feelings!*

- *I choose to be gentle, patient, and loving with myself.*

- *I am worthy of peace and joy.*

- *I am worthy of my dreams.*

6

The Power of Your Cultural Inheritance

It's Full of Bones!
If you take all the water out of the Atlantic Ocean
You will find a trail of human bones stretching from
Africa to the Americas
It's full of bones!
I know the legacy of slavery
Passed down from my great-grandparents, slaves themselves.
As children of the 1960s we united
And pumped stories of our ancestors' spilled blood
Into the heart of the Civil Rights Movement—
That blood, those stories gave us a new life.
It's full of bones!
But as we began to have individual opportunities,
Too many of us failed to tell those stories to our children.
I didn't want to—
I wanted to shield you from the pain I had always known.
But now that pain has become your reality
It's full of bones!

But the truth is . . .
Beyond all the pain past and present, we are still here.
We have within us a spirit so powerful—
It enables us not only to endure but also to overcome.
Come home to the truth of who we are.

As human beings we often define ourselves in relation to our cultural identity. Our ancestors, our culture can provide us with roots and a sense of belonging. When viewed properly, this sense of cultural identity can be a source of tremendous strength and power.

In the poem that opens this chapter, a father shares with his sons the power available to them through the suffering and overcoming of African-Americans from slavery to the present. He references the bones to underscore the idea that the very marrow of the bones, the genetic coding that passes from generation to generation, carries a legacy and a power.

Regardless of the labels of identity you choose to embrace (age, race, sex, class, or sexuality), there is a legacy of greatness available to you. This chapter is about tapping into the power of your ancestors and the legacy of your people in the world—this is your CULTURAL INHERITANCE.

Your CULTURAL INHERITANCE consists of the patterns of response and group behaviors you inherit/learn from the culture(s) with which you identify through both conscious and unconscious suggestion.

In my play *Emergency*, I tell the story of a slave ship that rises out of the Hudson River in front of the Statue of Liberty in present day New York City. For me, slavery represents the time of greatest bondage in our nation's history and the Statue of Liberty is our greatest symbol of freedom. There are even historical rumors that the Statue of Liberty was originally meant to be a monument to the end of slavery in America at the close of the Civil War and that the first draft of this statue was a figure of a black woman with a broken chain in one hand and another at her feet. I use the metaphor of the slave ship in front of the Statue of Liberty to ask the question, what stands in front of our freedom? Not just our physical freedom, but our mental, emotional, and spiritual freedom to be bold and fully expressed?

The poem that opens this chapter is spoken by Reginald, a black man who climbs aboard the slave ship and is possessed by the spirit of an ancestral African chief. In the play we discover that years earlier Reginald's wife was murdered by an urban black youth. To avoid the pain of his loss, he has escaped into the recesses of his mind and denied his identity as a black man. And he has chosen not to pass on to his children the legacy of African-Americans in this country. By the time he speaks the poem, the ancestral chief has empowered him to come home to the truth of who he is—to his Authentic Self. This empowerment enables Reginald to pass on to his children the truth of their Cultural Inheritance. And in this poem he passes that truth on to his children. That is the true gift of transforming your pain to power. We not only heal ourselves, but we become vessels for the healing of others. Consider Reginald's son Rodney's response to his father's transformation.

THE BONES, THEY BREATHE

Look at me on the outside, it seems I'm holding it together.
Walking through life just fine, no matter the weather.
But inside I'm stumbling—lost, broken, confused.
My heart's lost its beat, feels all mangled, abused.
Father, how do I construct the pieces of my manhood
When my model is crumbling before my eyes—
I'm missing peace in this puzzle; I'm losing hope in this game
And I don't want to pass debt to my children so I'm trying to
      reclaim all that's been lost.
But each time I reach I grasp a heart full of pain—
The pain I feel and the pain I see in so many of us sleepwalking
      these streets

In an unconscious state of emergency
And each day I fight and I try to wake up
And try to wake the sleepers who are sleeping while awake
So used to walking in weeds they got us thinkin' it's grass and
we smokin' it.
But Father when I heard you scream, "It's full of bones!"
Then I heard you speak about the truth of who we are
Hope . . . like a ray of light exploded in the depths of me
And BANG! It's waking me up
And I'm emerging from a deep sleep—see—
I'm in a state of emergence-see—
And as I emerge I see . . . my missing peace has always been
in me
And my choice to reach past this nightmare reality into the
marrow of my bones
I am in a state of emergence-see—
And as I emerge I see our very bones know an ancient
divinity:
And our bones, our bones, our bones they breathe:
One simple question: to be or not to be?
Shall we die or shall we dare to live FREE?
Father, I choose life! I choose to tell the story!
For beyond pain that makes hope seem impossible
Our bones, our bones, our bones they breathe:
In this world we may be bound but our spirits are free
Our bones, our bones, our bones they breathe:

We can overcome if we change the way we see
See ourselves, see our past, see our possibility
Our bones, our bones, our bones they breathe:
We are the essence of liberty!
We are the breath of divinity!
We are family!
We must not die!
We must not sleep!
We must wake up!
Wake up and DREAM!

Like Reginald and his son Rodney, we can all be healed and empowered by our Cultural Inheritance. Whatever labels of identity you choose to embrace—race, class, age, sex, or sexuality—there are models of greatness for those labels. And that greatness is available to you as inspiration and power through presence with your Authentic Self.

At the deepest knowing of our Authentic Self we discover that we are all one.

And at the deepest knowing of our Authentic Self we discover that we are all one—we are all the same unlimited potential to create, do, or be *anything*. That means you can embrace any great person who has ever lived as part of your Cultural Inheritance. Think about it, aren't there people of vastly different backgrounds who inspire you? Still, we live in a world of labels and categorizations. And when we choose to be empowered rather than limited by those labels, an abundance of inspiration becomes available to us through the power of our Cultural Inheritance.

As an African-American, I take pride in the history of the African in America, of being a resilient overcomer. In the summer of 2000, I was invited to Ghana to sing at the Opening Night ceremony of PANAFEST—when Africans from across the diaspora gather at the Cape Coast Castle in Ghana for a festival of remembrance. The Cape Coast Castle is a gorgeous white castle on the ocean. It is also one of the largest slave dungeons where West Africans were kept before boarding the slave ships. The following monologue spoken by the character Kwesi from my play *Emergency* paints a vivid picture of the horror of these slave dungeons.

As a slave-ologist, slave dungeons are my specialty. The slave dungeons you are about to see are the largest facility where the Africans were kept during the Transatlantic Slave Trade. As our tour begins, we here at the Slave Dungeons ask that you leave your rage and pain at the entrance gate because there is enough inside. Thank you and please follow me.

(As he turns, he becomes an African woman searching for her missing husband who has been captured. She speaks in Ga—a West African language—a breathless plea for God's help.)

Me da wase me yon ku pon. Me da wase me Kwesi . . . me Kwesi.

(To crowd.)

We have just entered the courtyard where the Africans were first brought in chains after being captured from their neighboring villages. Here, they stood in the broiling sun while they were inspected by the Dutch Masters. Thank you and please follow me.

(As he turns upstage, his hands cross violently above his head as if chained. Enraged, he speaks the following words of resistance to an imaginary guard.)

Olokikijulu amanla owetu! Olokikijulu amanla owetu!

(To crowd.)

We have now entered the Slave Dungeons where the Africans were kept. Here, they defecated on the same floor where they slept and ate. You notice to your right a set of stairs. They lead to the Master's quarters. The African women would be led up the stairs and then raped by the Master. Thank you and please follow me.

(As he turns upstage, he becomes an African woman being raped by the Master. She weeps the following words . . .)

Me da wase me yon ku pon. Me da wase me Africa . . . me Africa.

(To crowd. He walks downstage as he says the following . . .)

We have now reached the final room of our tour. This is where the Africans were brought before they boarded slave ships like Remembrance *for the passage to America. Here, you notice a small rectangular window—the Gate of No Return. By the time the Africans—the slaves—reached this point, they were so small and weak they could fit through this small rectangular window . . . my brothers and sisters, the time has come . . . we have arrived at the end of our tour.*

At the Opening Night ceremony of PANAFEST 2000, thousands of African descendants from across the diaspora gathered all dressed in white. We walked through the village each carrying a lighted candle. As we arrived at the entrance to the slave dungeons, I had the opportunity to sing the spiritual "Lord, How Come Me Here?"

Lord, how come me here?
Lord, how come me here?
Oh, Lord, how come me here?
I wish I never was born . . .

Then we took a nighttime tour of the slave dungeons. As I walked through the cold, dark stone dungeons, I could literally feel the pain of those who had suffered unspeakable cruelty in this place centuries before. I wept in remembrance of the pain they experienced and for the trauma that had been passed on.

You see, just as there can be a positive or negative Mental

and Emotional Inheritance, there can also be a positive and negative Cultural Inheritance. I firmly believe that so many of the challenges faced by members of the African-American community can be traced back to unhealed wounds from the legacy of slavery. This concept could be a book unto itself, but let's explore it briefly. For too many African-Americans the shackles of slavery that once chained our bodies are still enslaving our hearts and minds. And to be clear, I am not just speaking of the socioeconomic disparities. A person can have a Ph.D. and a six-figure income and still be enslaved to his or her thoughts and emotions.

There are also several extremely urgent economic and social disparities facing the African-American community and our nation as a whole that need to be addressed. And I believe many of these disparities are rooted in the legacy of slavery in this country and the history of the African in America. Our children are being dropped every day by poverty, failing educational systems, a lack of access to quality health care, and the absence of safe homes. I believe a core step in the healing of our nation is for all those interested in justice and healing to first know the truth of their Authentic Self, and then, to remember the power of their positive Cultural Inheritance. Yes, I said, positive. For you see, even though the African-American community and many other people around the world have experienced tremendous obstacles and challenges, there has also been tremendous bravery and overcoming. The suffering of those who came before has not been in vain. Instead, the gifts our ancestors gave, often with their lives, provide a model for the tenacity and power that is always possible, and the responsibility to dream new dreams.

Consider this poem from my play *Mr. Joy*, spoken by a fifteen-year-old black teenager named DeShawn.

A Black Boy Speaks

You tell me to pull up my pants, pull down my hoodie,
And watch the words I speak,
The roots of this system are poisoned and you focusing on
*   a leaf?*
I understand that witnessing my breakdown brings tears to
*   your eyes,*
But I'm crying too, can you hear me?
There are reasons for my demise:
Maybe just maybe I call my boy, "my nigga"
'Cause we out here living like slaves
And maybe I act so angry
'Cause that's how the forgotten always behaves—
These projects are our plantation
And rage at our condition keeps us in chains.
Why don't you Harriet Tubman us to freedom
Instead of shaming us for our pain?
Our Underground Railroad's been derailed
And we stranded without a ride,
How am I supposed to be a man with no father as a guide?

*Most children learn how to behave from what they see their
    parents do,*
*And a history untold repeats itself so is some of the blame
    on you?*
*All of a sudden just out of nowhere there's a generation of lost
    black boys?*
*No. The systematic destruction of a people is loud—it makes
    a lot of noise—*
Why didn't you hear our screams—
When Hopelessness caught us in its net?
They've thrown us in the belly of this ghetto slave ship
And told us to forget
Our hopes, our dreams, any vision of a better life,
We've been captured and our Middle Passage is rife
*With the stench of poverty and horrific screams of
    self-doubt—*
They've chained our hearts and minds—
Is it any wonder we can't find our way out?
*Create a search party and come find us for we are desperate
    to be found.*
*How do we escape to freedom because we agree that we are
    bound?*
*How do we say no to the Jim Crow of these prisons every-
    where?*
Half of us are going there and most folks don't seem to care—
How did you organize before to obtain our Civil Rights?

*'Cause we need a Revolution now—teach us the right way to
    fight.*
*We've been fighting all our lives—we just weren't given the
    right tools—*
Most of us want to learn
But have you seen the state of these so-called schools?
A black boy speaks—will you hear my cry?
*Or will you just continue to live your life while day after day
    we die?*

Despite the horror of the legacy of slavery, there is incredible strength and empowerment that can be gathered from that legacy, as chronicled in DeShawn's poem.

In the spring of 2007, I had the opportunity to take a private tour of the American I Am exhibit in Los Angeles with the legendary actor Sidney Poitier. This exhibit chronicled the journey of the African in America from slavery to the present. I was blessed to walk side by side with this giant of a man who was pleasantly surprised to see himself pictured several times in the exhibit, for his portrayals in *A Raisin in the Sun* and for his Oscar-award-winning performance in *Lilies of the Field*. As we journeyed through these big moments in African-American history, he shared with me stories of his friendships with the many artists and leaders who graced the walls.

Eventually, we arrived at an exhibit that reflected the slave experience, and there was an actual Door of No Return from the

Cape Coast Slave Dungeon in Ghana. Images from my trip to PANAFEST 2000 immediately flashed through my mind's eye. Mr. Poitier reached out and touched the door, and then he instructed me to touch the door. Then he said, "This is wood; it is living, breathing energy. So many have passed through this door, and as we both touch this door, I pass the best of what I am to you." Mr. Poitier in that moment provided me with a profound understanding of my positive Cultural Inheritance.

Similarly, I have been blessed to develop a very close relationship with Ruby Dee and her husband Ossie Davis before he passed. Miss Dee and Mr. Davis are the epitome of the Artist/Activist and they have hosted many Civil Rights Leaders in their home, including Dr. King, Malcolm X, and their families. Ruby Dee and Ossie Davis used the platform of their celebrity to speak out and create awareness for countless causes.

After attending an early performance of my solo play *Emergency* in New York City in the summer of 2005, Miss Dee made it part of her mission to create a platform for my work. She even presented me in a theater in Harlem and insisted that the new artistic director of the renowned Public Theater attend. She packed the seven-hundred-seat theater and gave me a remarkable introduction. The audience was electric and leapt to their feet at the end of the performance. At the reception immediately following, the artistic director of the Public Theater, Oskar Eustis, offered me my first off-Broadway contract on the spot.

When the play was reviewed, one *New York Times* reviewer made some negative comments. Miss Dee had already read the review when I called her devastated. I was fully prepared to have a pity party and go off about how unjust and unfair the review had been. She absolutely refused me any space for those negative thoughts and feelings. She simply said, "We have always had to dance with a gun at our feet. Still we dance." She went on to celebrate my work in the play and its value.

The following day Miss Dee and I had an interview on Whoopie Goldberg's radio show to publicize the show. When I arrived at the radio station, Miss Dee had several postcards in her lap. Once we were on the air, she began to read from the postcards—they were positive quotes about the play from various reviews. Yet Miss Dee only chose to read quotes from the *New York Times*—the very review I was so hurt and incensed by. She read several positive quotes from this review over the airways to tens of thousands of people.

At the end I asked her, "Miss Dee, with all the completely positive press for the show, why did you choose to only read from that one mixed review?" She responded, "He may have said some negative things, but all those listeners will never know it. We take what is useful and we discard the rest." This wisdom was the product of years of struggle and overcoming at the forefront of the civil rights movement as an Artist/Activist. In her words and her actions, she provided me with the Cultural Inheritance that when you are boldly living your truth and fighting for the liberation of others, there will always be some people who will try to belittle you or take you down, but you decide how you respond. You can choose to take what is useful and discard the rest.

EXERCISE:
Embracing Your Cultural Inheritance

Again, your Cultural Inheritance consists of the patterns of response and group behaviors you inherit/learn from the culture(s) with which you identify through both conscious and unconscious suggestion.

Please take out your notebook and answer the following questions:

1. What are some aspects of your Cultural Inheritance you observed in your larger community growing up?

2. How did you feel and think about the quality of life of people whom you identified as part of your culture growing up?

3. How did these thoughts and feelings about your culture impact how you felt about what might be possible for yourself?

4. Now make a distinction for yourself between what aspects of your Cultural Inheritance empower you and what aspects of your Cultural Inheritance limit you. Can you identify the impact your Cultural Inheritance has had on your life?

Through the power of your Authentic Self you can choose to use the aspects of your Cultural Inheritance that empower you and discard what limits you.

STATEMENTS OF AFFIRMATION

- ✦ I have a rich Cultural Inheritance.

- ✦ Though there is some pain in the story of my people, there is also immense overcoming.

- ✦ My ancestors suffered so I would not have to.

- ✦ I stand on the shoulders of giants.

- ✦ Through presence with my Authentic Self, I choose to be empowered by all they sacrificed.

- ✦ I have agency and power in my life.

- ✦ I am proclaiming my ability to transform my pain to power.

- ✦ I understand that in the process of my healing, some negative, painful experiences and memories will emerge.

- ✦ I allow the space for my thoughts and feelings, even though they may be painful, because I know that my intention is to create the life of my dreams.

- ✦ I boldly proclaim:

  - • *I am powerful!*

- *I am greater than my past!*

- *I am greater than any negative thoughts or feelings!*

- *I choose to be gentle, patient, and loving with myself.*

- *I am worthy of peace and joy.*

- *I am worthy of my dreams.*

7

The Power of Gratitude and Affirmative Speaking

For years, I lived in resentment toward my father for his abandonment. I thought how selfish it was of him to choose his addiction over his family, over me. Then one day it occurred to me: I am who I am largely because my father was who he was. Now, sure, I had to survive and heal without his support or presence, but the wound that was created by his choices is actually a very fertile place out of which I create. All of the earthly angels who have stepped into my life in the space of his absence have taught me lessons that he simply was not prepared to teach. All of the mistakes I made out of my pain, all of the times I got it wrong, fell, had to father myself, brush myself off, and try again, all of these experiences strengthened me and gave me a story to tell. And in this way, I am who I am because my father was exactly who he was. In this way, I have reasons to be grateful. In the most challenging aspects of our lives, there is a way to perceive the challenges through the lens of gratitude. When we know our Authentic Self, we have the power to choose how we perceive any situation.

Now that we have unpacked the limiting thoughts, feelings, and other inheritances from our past, it is time to be intentional about creating the lives of our dreams. Being present with our Authentic Self is about remembering our power to choose moment to moment how we will view our lives.

At any point we can choose to focus on what has gone wrong in our lives, what hasn't worked, what we wish could be better. Or at any moment we can choose to be grateful for the miracles in our lives. We can choose to celebrate the survivors we are, how much we have overcome, and the life that is still available to us. At any moment we can choose the POWER OF GRATITUDE.

One of the most dynamic tools for transforming our pain to power is Gratitude.

GRATITUDE is the choice to feel appreciation for the things and people in one's life.

I have spent a tremendous amount of time meeting with and reading the stories of high-achieving people. Gratitude is a constant theme. No matter how aspirational these high achievers may be, the space of giving thanks for what they have in the moment provides an opening for even greater success. If you want to make a million dollars and you presently only make twenty thousand, the space of true gratitude for what you have is an opening for abundance. If you want ten friends and you only have one, the space of true gratitude for the one friend creates the opening for other friends to enter.

> In the most challenging aspects of our lives, there is a way to perceive the challenges through the lens of gratitude.

Gratitude is a magnetic force. Gratitude activates the law of attraction. When we are grateful, we vibrate joyously at the frequency of that which we desire, and that joyous vibration brings more of what we desire to us. When we practice gratitude, we breathe more deeply, our minds are clearer, our hearts more open.

No matter the circumstance, there are always reasons to be grateful. No matter how challenging your life may have been, you are a miracle. Why? You are still here to tell the story. You have the impetus, the courage to read a book focused on healing and empowerment. You haven't given up. You haven't lost your mind. You are a survivor. You still have breath in your lungs. And wherever there is breath, there is life and there is hope. And now you know the truth of your Authentic Self.

No matter how discouraged we may feel in those moments when our past stories haunt us, we can choose to breathe and feel the air pass through our nostrils and into our lungs, and be grateful for the breath of life. There is always sky and trees and ocean and birds and smiling faces and possibility. There are miracles all around us when we choose to see them.

EXERCISE:
Miracle Moments

Even if an experience was extremely painful and challenging, you can still choose to view it as a miracle moment because you survived it—you are still here! You own your story and your right to tell it. Your story does not own you.

Please take out your notebook and complete the following steps.

1. Write down three moments in your life when you absolutely thought that you couldn't make it through.

2. How did you make it through each of the experiences? How was each experience ultimately resolved?

3. What did you discover about yourself and life in each of these experiences?

EXERCISE:
Gratitude Pages

Please put on one of your favorite pieces of upbeat music. This should be a song you absolutely love that makes you feel good about yourself and life in general. Put the song on repeat. Now take out your notebook and write a list of everything you can think of for which you are grateful. If you don't know where to begin, start with your breath—for breath is life, breath is possibility, breath is choice. Think of the people who love you. Think of every big or small happy moment in your life. It could be as simple as your favorite color or food. It could be the love of your life. Write until your wrist hurts. Go ahead and write before continuing to read.

How do you feel right now, in this moment, after completing your gratitude pages? No matter what challenges you may be facing, there are always reasons to be grateful. It is a simple concept, but sometimes the decision to choose gratitude when there are so many reasons to be upset can be a challenging one. But choosing gratitude immediately makes life brighter. It immediately reminds us that no matter how challenging things may be at times, there are always reasons to be grateful.

THE POWER OF AFFIRMATIVE SPEAKING

Passion creates Action. When you know your Authentic Self, you have the ability to use your thoughts and emotions to create your reality. Now I would like to empower you to continue the process of creating the life of your dreams through passionate AFFIRMATIVE SPEAKING.

*"In the beginning was the word, and the word was with God,
And the word was God."*

—THE BIBLE, JOHN 1:1

In the previous chapters, I have discussed in detail my insecurities about everything, ranging from my ability to be different than my father and brother to my belief in my own attractiveness. Today, I know my future is unlimited and I celebrate my attractiveness. I have arrived at this place largely through practicing Affirmative Speaking.

As silly as it may sound to some people and as awkward as it may feel, I have stood in front of mirrors all over this world and in moments of insecurity looked deeply into my own eyes and spoken power to my pain. I have stood in front of my bathroom mirror completely naked and looked at my body—all of its "imperfections"—and traced with my eyes every feature from my nose to my toes and told myself each was beautiful. I have done this when I did not believe it. I have done this when I hated the way I looked. I have spoken affirmative thoughts to myself time and time again, until I eventually began to believe them.

In moments of great opportunity, when I have been afraid before a major performance or business meeting, I have snuck into a dressing room or a bathroom and looked deeply into my own eyes and said, "You've got this. You are prepared. You are destined for greatness. God is with you. You have something to say, you have something to give."

At moments when I've gotten lost in the maze of past pain, when I felt regrets for mistakes I made or frustration over days of joy that I lost, I have stopped, noticed what I was thinking, and begun quietly feeding myself affirmative thoughts. I have done this lying in bed at night, in the back of taxis, sharing a meal with other people, even on stage in front of thousands of people.

During moments when I did not want to be alive because even after years of therapy and doing the spiritual work, I still had moments of feeling insecure, I've had to encourage myself with the power of my Affirmative Speaking. Affirmative Speaking to myself about myself and my own possibility has literally saved my life time and time again, and it continues to give me that quality of life I truly desire on a daily basis.

I wish I could tell you that there is one cure-all for our past pain. I wish I could tell you that once we know the truth of our Authentic Self we always remember it. I wish I could tell you that once we have an experience of deep joy and possibility it never leaves us. That has not been my experience. Today, I have more joyous moments than I have ever had, and I have them because I choose them day by day, sometimes moment by moment.

With power, passion, and clarity proclaim the truth of who you are.

I firmly believe that Affirmative Speaking is one of the most life-transforming tools you can employ. With power, passion, and clarity proclaim the truth of who you are. Stand in front of a mirror and look deeply into your own eyes and proclaim how wonderful and amazing you are. Take off your clothes, stand in front of a mirror, and trace with your eyes every aspect of your face, of your body, and proclaim your own attractiveness. Insist that your mind and your heart agree with the truth of your Authentic Self. Why not? In different cultures and throughout different periods of time, every body type you can imagine and every type of feature you can think of has been celebrated or considered most beautiful. You are a special, gorgeous, dynamic creation just as you are right now in this moment. Anyone or anything (including your own thoughts and feelings) telling you otherwise is lying.

Certainly, we all have aspects of ourselves we would like to shift, but let's start from a place of gratitude for who and what we are right now in this moment. Then, if we choose to shift anything in our lives, let's do it from a place of love and celebration of self. There is no lack, there is no limitation unless you choose to believe there is.

EXERCISE:
Statements of Affirmation

Our words have creative power. Begin to fill in your Statements of Affirmation with your wildest dreams of what you would like to create for your life:

◆ Understanding and knowing my Authentic Self:

- Who I am is the Unlimited Potential to Create, Be, Do ANYTHING.

- Who I am is a person who _____ [fill in your dream/aspiration]

✦ Through the Power of my Authentic Self, I declare:

- I have thoughts. I have feelings. I am not my thoughts. I am not my feelings.

✦ My Authentic Self is a parent to my thoughts and feelings.

✦ Now that I understand and know my Authentic Self:

- I choose thoughts that empower me.

- I choose emotions that cause me to feel good about myself.

✦ I have experiences but I am not defined or limited by my experiences.

✦ I have a past, but I am not defined or limited by my past.

✦ When I am present with my Authentic Self, I can use my past experiences to empower me.

✦ I am limitless.

Now I want to invite you to go to a mirror and speak these words to yourself with emotion, power, and enthusiasm. It may seem silly at first, but just go with it. Allow yourself to embrace a spirit of playfulness. How bold can you be? How committed can you be? How much can you believe in your power to manifest your dreams now that you know the truth of your Authentic Self through the power of Affirmative Speaking? Go for it! Be bold! Have fun!

EXERCISE:
Manifesto

The highest form of using Affirmative Speaking to create the life of one's dream is to write your Manifesto.

A Manifesto is a written public declaration of the intentions, motives, or views of the issuer, be it an individual, group, political party, or government. It is often political in nature, but it may present an individual's life stance. "Manifesto" is derived from the Italian word *manifesto*, itself derived from the Latin *manifestum*, meaning "clear" or "conspicuous," which means "obvious to the eye or mind." So let's be clear, let's be conspicuous. It's time to write your Manifesto.

Please take out your notebook and complete the following statements referring to your earlier notes.

1. My Initial Breakdown was

2. My Resulting Thought Pattern was

3. My Dominating Emotional Landscape was

4. I inherited from my core community the thoughts

5. I inherited from my core community the feelings

6. The Resulting Behavior Pattern was

7. The impact of this is . . .

Once you have completed this section, please take a moment to include the following statements of affirmation to ground yourself in your purpose and intent in creating this Manifesto.

+ *I understand this part of my story—a story that I own—a story that I have the power to rewrite.*

+ *I have thoughts; I am not my thoughts. I have feelings; I am not my feelings.*

+ *Who I am is the unlimited potential to create, do, or be anything.*

Now that you have clarified your past and grounded yourself in your purpose, it is time to create the future by continuing to write your Manifesto:

8. My chosen Thought Pattern is

9. My chosen Emotional Landscape is

10. My chosen Primary Behavior Pattern is

11. The impact of this is

8

The Power of Vision and Faith

Despite my mother's best efforts to raise us without a father, when I was ten, my older brother became addicted to crack cocaine. My brother is ten years older than me—a child from my mother's previous relationship, before she met my father. My mother refused to give up on him, and he remained with us in the house while in the throes of his addiction. So much of my growing up was shaped by my brother's addiction. One evening, my brother was high and held the family at gunpoint. When he wasn't paying attention, I escaped up the stairs and called the cops. I remember my mother collapsing in my arms and my endeavoring to carry her up the stairs as my brother raced into the basement and the cops charged after him.

My brother's addiction also caused me to feel a great deal of fear as a child. Because my mother worked such long hours, I was often at the house alone with my brother. I would dread returning home after school. My first action would be to evaluate my brother's emotional state and then I would gorge myself with food to suppress the fear I was feeling.

Crack cocaine is an ugly drug, and sometimes my brother would become violent and I would run across the street to a neighbor's house or to the church and wait until my mother got home from work.

I remember one particular time, when I was ten, I escaped from the house and ran to the church, and something stopped me in my tracks in the church parking lot. I closed my eyes, and I saw myself as a grown man wearing all black and I was standing on the stage of an amphitheater in front of tens of thousands of people speaking to them. As I child, I was not certain what was happening, but I know I felt encouraged and began to believe there was something possible for my life behind the difficulty of my surroundings. I believe there are Divine gifts in life, and this vision certainly proved to be one of them in my life. Through the power of this vision I began to understand, even at ten years old, that there was a purpose to the chaos and confusion I was experiencing. There have been numerous moments of doubt and difficulty in my life when that vision has encouraged me.

This experience taught me at an early age the POWER OF VISION—of having a dream. It helped save my life. Everyone may not have experienced a vision like I did as a child, but at any point we can choose to create a vision for ourselves. It is simply a process of taking the time to be honest with ourselves about what we really, truly want for our lives and crafting a vivid picture in our mind's eye of how we will feel, and how we will exist on a day-to-day basis in our lives, once we have it.

A VISION is a vivid image of your life that you choose to embrace and reference to empower you to realize your unlimited potential and manifest your dreams.

Upon reflection, my vision in the church parking lot—the vision that would guide me for the rest of my life—may have been inspired by watching a video of Dr. Martin Luther King, Jr.'s "I Have a Dream" speech. I was in third grade when my teacher Mavis Jackson showed the class Dr. King's speech, and a whole world of possibility opened up for me. Here was this man standing in front of tens of thousands of people using words to inspire and change the world. And he was black like me. I wanted to be able to do that! Dr. King made me aware of my love for words and provided me with a MODEL OF POSSIBILITY. Sometimes if a positive role model is not available in the home, we have to find it outside the home.

A MODEL OF POSSIBILITY is a chosen role model and source of inspiration that reflects your highest vision of yourself and empowers you to manifest that vision.

I rushed to Ms. Jackson and proclaimed boldly, "I want to do that! I want to write speeches like Dr. King." And she began to help me. She was another Model of Possibility. She gave me advice and helped me write my first speeches. Teachers, mentors, and advisors have played key roles in helping me transform my pain to power.

As a ten-year-old child, I began to give speeches all over my hometown of Dayton, Ohio, at churches and for social organizations like the NAACP and the Urban League. Each time I gave a speech, I poured all my heart and soul into it. And the word began to spread. By the time I was in sixth grade, I was traveling the country giving speeches. Despite my chaotic home life, I found something that I loved and I had a Vision and a Model of Possibility that empowered me to believe that a dream greater than my present reality was possible. Vision and a commitment to excellence were my bridge over incarceration, poverty, and disenfranchisement.

The Power of Vision is a core aspect of transforming our pain to power. In the previous chapters, we discussed how we often color our future with past pain. Now that we have taken our past out of our future, our future is a blank canvas that we have the power to paint with all the beauty we can imagine.

What do you envision for your life? What is your dream? When was the last time you sat down and asked yourself, "What do I want? What do I *really* want?" If there were no barriers, what is the wildest dream you could imagine for yourself? How do you see yourself a month from now, six months from now, a year, five years, a decade? What do you want?

Now that you know the truth of your Authentic Self, your future is truly unlimited. Sure, it is a moment-to-moment process to create that future, but this process starts with a vision.

It is never too late to dream, to envision new possibilities for yourself.

I would like to encourage you to spend some time daydreaming. Allow your wildest imaginings to come to life as vivid pictures in your mind. Who in your life do you admire? Who do you see at work, on television, in movies, and say, "I would love to have a life like that"? What regrets still tiptoe around the recesses of your heart? "Oh, I wish I had gotten my college degree." "I wish I had learned to play that instrument or taken singing lessons." "I always wanted to go to cooking school or open a restaurant." Why not? When I was an undergraduate, there was a sixty-eight-year-old woman in my class who was getting her college degree. It is never too late to dream, to envision new possibilities for yourself. People do the extraordinary every single day. Why not you? You are extraordinary. You are the unlimited potential to create, do, or be *anything* through presence with your Authentic Self.

EXERCISE:
Vision & Model of Possibility—A Vision Board

I'm going to ask you to do a little craft project right now. This might seem juvenile to you at first, but I encourage you to just try it. You're going to need a large white poster board, glue, and magazines full of images that excite you, images of houses or cars or bodies you would love to have or places you would love to travel. Spend some time thinking about everything you could ever imagine and dream for your life. If the list is very long, narrow it down to about ten things. Find images of those ten things you want, cut them out, and glue them to the board. Allow yourself to be playful with this process. Be sure to include some Models of Possibilities—images of people who embody what you envision/desire for your own life.

Images are very powerful tools to manifesting our dreams. It is one thing to write your dreams in words, but you can gain a greater level of clarity and inspiration when you see images of your dreams right before your eyes. I would encourage you to place your Vision Board somewhere that you can reference often. Perhaps you can write in a time in your calendar when you will revisit the board to see how you are progressing toward your dreams. I would suggest checking in at least once a week initially.

Also, seeing images of other people who have what you want says to your mind and heart, "If they can have it, so can I." In a world that moves so quickly and is full of so much visual stimulation, this Vision Board can also be a grounding force to remind you with absolute clarity of what you are endeavoring to create for yourself through the power of your Authentic Self.

THE POWER OF FAITH

In my play *Mr. Joy*, Bessie passes on her understanding of faith to her granddaughter Clarissa with these words:

> *Baby, we can't always focus on what we see,*
> *That's why we need to sprinkle faith,*
> *You see, faith, it's a substance—*
> *It's the substance of things hoped for.*
> *Faith is like a magic dust—*
> *And you can sprinkle it over your doubts and your fears,*
> *And Faith, it turns them into possibilities, into dreams.*
> *Clarissa, baby, I sprinkle faith over your life every night*
> *   when I pray.*
> *You want a happy ending? You can have one—*
> *Just take all your fears and sprinkle them with Faith—*
> *It's the substance of things hoped for.*

It is never a question of what is possible. It is a question of what you can believe. Faith that does not waver cannot fail. The POWER OF FAITH is another crucial component of transforming our pain to power.

FAITH is the substance of things hoped for, the evidence of things not seen.

This definition of faith is a direct quote from the Bible. When you hope for something, faith is the space between that internal hope and its external manifestation. The space between your desire and its physical manifestation is the space of faith. When we have an internal vision of the future we would like to manifest for ourselves, but we do not yet have the external manifestation of that vision, faith is the evidence that our greatest dreams are not only possible but inevitable. Do you have faith? What or whom do you have faith in? How do you define faith? What exists in the space between your desires and their manifestation?

It is never a question of what is possible. It is a question of what you can believe.

Earlier in this book, I stated that the concept of the Authentic Self is not a religious belief or concept but that it is compatible with many different religious or spiritual beliefs. My journey as a Christian has been a source of tremendous empowerment for me. For me, the Authentic Self is parallel with the Spirit of Christ within, which I view as an enabling force that empowers me to be loving and generous toward myself and others, and to accomplish my greatest dreams. I access the spirit of Christ through breath—the breath of life.

For people of other faiths, the Authentic Self may also be called the Buddha consciousness or presence with Allah. At their best, the concepts in this book are a practical contemporary application of ancient spiritual principles that are compatible across a myriad of religious and spiritual beliefs.

Some people may be thinking, *Well, I don't have much faith. How can I have faith when all I have experienced is disappointment?* My question to you is this: What's the alternative? If we live a life without faith, without hope, we have no choice but to wander aimlessly in our past pain. There are a myriad of places to find faith, from spiritual communities, to nature, to the arts, to people, to books and beyond. The very fact that you have picked up this book and read to this point is proof of your faith—faith in yourself to keep trying, to keep believing that something more is possible for you.

Regardless of your spiritual or religious faith, you can choose to know that there is a power at your core that is greater than any limiting thoughts, feelings, or inheritances. By being present with this power within, you have the ability to create more joy in the world for yourself and for others.

For ultimately, Vision and Faith are not just for ourselves. Vision and Faith empower us to be a support and inspiration to others. Vision and Faith empower us to believe that the seemingly impossible is possible. Consider Bessie's prayer from my play

Mr. Joy as she pleads for the healing of her community that is wracked with violence.

A Grandmother's Prayer

For our angry, forgotten children, afraid, lost without hope
This Grandmother's Prayer we utter for you . . .
With wrinkled hands and weakened knees we kneel to pray,
And from the depths of our bellies groan for you . . .
Oh, Heavenly Father, forget not your angry children, afraid,
    lost without hope
Snatch them from the belly of the Beast,
Reach down from Heaven—gather them in Your mighty
    arms,
Embrace them with the strength of a Father's love,
Oh, You father to the fatherless,
Rip from their faces the masks of rage they wear to hide their
    fears,
Shine Your light on their true beauty and let them know
    that they are safe.
Safe even when their hearts are breaking,
Safe even when their prayers seem to go unanswered,
Safe even when hopelessness is all their earthly eyes can see—
Safe because they are your children too and if children then
    heirs:
Heirs to a boundless Inheritance beyond this earthly plane,
But while on this earth their bodies dwell,

We cry out to you, oh Father, shower them with Your Grace
Oh, we cry this Grandmother's Prayer.

In the midst of the deep sorrow Bessie feels around the condition of the young people in her community, it is her faith in a loving, powerful God that empowers her to keep going. Her faith empowers her to believe that despite the evidence, healing is possible. Her faith empowers her to take a stand for the healing of others. In the distance between the brokenness she witnesses in her community and the healing she envisions, Bessie stands in faith. And similarly, once you get clear about what you envision for yourself and others, the Power of Faith can sustain you and empower you to make that vision a reality.

9

The Power of Purpose

had just completed graduate school at the American Conservatory Theater in San Francisco, and I arrived in New York City ready to take over the world. I arrived in late August 2001. Two weeks later it was September 11 and the World Trade Center collapsed. It was a chaotic time, but in many ways New York City was at a standstill, and I did not find my place in the entertainment business immediately. In fact, I had trouble finding any place at all.

I was in a state of utter confusion. I had done the right things, played by the rules. I went to the best schools. I worked extremely hard while I was there. All of my teachers and mentors had the highest aspirations for me. But I just did not fit. No agent wanted to represent me. I couldn't even get a job as a waiter. I literally put in about thirty applications at various restaurants.

Eventually, a very close friend (really like my second mother), Julia Hobart, was able to get an interview for me to be a teaching artist with a phenomenal program called DreamYard. A teaching artist is a professional creative or performing artist who teaches his craft to students who are often not professionals.

I began teaching acting, singing, and writing in some of the most economically challenged areas in Brooklyn, Harlem, and the Bronx. By this time I had received the best education possible and traveled the US, Europe, and Africa as a writer/performer, and here I was encountering young people who were experiencing some of the exact same experiences I had growing up. So many of my students had family members who were in prison or addicts. I remember a time I kept a young girl after class because she was really misbehaving, only to discover her father had shot her mother then shot himself in front of her. Over the course of four years, I worked in literally dozens of schools interacting with thousands of young people through DreamYard and other arts education programs. My heart became full with the stories of these young people and their parents, as well as my fellow teachers and administrators. Sometimes being in these schools felt like walking through a war zone, with students literally hearing gunshots right outside the classroom and dropping beneath their desks. Once a man was shot right outside our classroom, and the students had to walk around the chalk imprint of his deceased body to exit the building. Classrooms were overcrowded with too few resources. I wondered, *How can this be the state of our education system? Is this the best we can do for our children?*

My growing up in chaos, then receiving the best education possible, and then returning as a teacher to chaotic communities like the one in which I had grown up clarified my purpose and prompted me to create the work I do now. I began to question why so many of the people I knew were having so many problems and why things weren't changing. I developed an immense sense of urgency around the world our children are presently living in and the world we are leaving for them. I wanted to explore how we could look these problems straight in the face in a way that would be bearable, address what is going on, and ultimately transform these problems, transform this pain to power.

I also began to understand the vision I had as a little boy standing in the parking lot of that church. I knew that it was time to bring all the parts of myself together. I explore this process of discovery in the following poem from my play *Emergency*.

Duality Duel—An Autobiography of Personal Insanity

There's a battle going on inside of me
Between my well-crafted external persona
And an internal force trying to break free—
It's battle, you see, between the Nerd and the Nigga in me.
Can the Nerd and the Nigga co-exist?
They goin' have to, Nerd—
But, Nigga, it doesn't make sense,
I didn't spend four years in the Ivy League

Learning how to think, talk, and feel
In order to jump into a rage every time they try and kill me.
But the truth is, Nerd, I've always been around
When that poison ivy bull crap was beating yo' butt down,
These strong arms, they held you, told you not to feel it,
Gave you time enough to heal it and become a nerd again.
But, Nigga, all you seem to feel is rage,
And that will keep me out of their circles
And off the front page of the *New York Times* and the
    Daily News
Not if you shoot somebody!
And that's my point: you are more than that cold, stony
    glare,
Those weighty Timberlands, and that nappy hair—
Aw, hold up, now—
No, listen, Nigga, that rage, it's like a cage that keeps
    love out
And you in jail burning in nigga thug nigga hell—
Aw, shut up, Nerd, you ain't heard a word I said.
I gotta smack you upside yo' well-brushed head?
Without me there is no you—
Now, wait a second, Nigga, let's talk this through—
Naw, Nerd, journey to the Nigga in you!
I been silent long enough, got yo' butt through school
Gave you time enough to learn their rules,
Now the time has come for you to pay yo' dues
'Cause these little kids in the street, they need you.

But they think they can't relate 'cause you act all removed.
When the truth is, Nerd, what they are is you,
'Cause no matta how hard you try
To deny the way you think, talk, and feel.
Yo' daddy still smokes heroin,
Yo' brother's still on crack,
Ghetto nightmares still haunt yo' dreams
And yo' mama is still black.
I ain't sayin' you gotta become me but this one thing is true
Inside you is a hard Nigga you gotta let come through
'Cause this assimilatin' bull crap will surely beat you down,
And if you choke me long enough, my Nerd, I will not stick
  around.
Put the strut back in yo' walk, say what you really feel
Be all of you so all of us can heal.
The time for the lyin' and denyin' is through
It's time, Nerd, journey to the Nigga in you!

I began to discover that rather than running from my past, I could use the lessons of my past to empower others. I was no longer the terrified boy certain he would follow in the footsteps of his father and brother and inherit their addiction and incarceration. I was no longer the insecure young man who didn't believe in my own attractiveness or self-worth. I was a survivor. I had been through the dark night of the soul time and time again and I was still here. A part of me believed that I had to deny my past—what I had survived. I had to act, talk, walk, and dress like someone who had graduated from Yale, gone to one of the top acting training programs, and sung opera in Aspen and across Europe. A part of me believed that I had to act like I was born with a silver spoon in my mouth.

But when I entered these classrooms in some of the most economically challenged areas of Brooklyn, Harlem, and the Bronx and saw the eyes of so many young people desperate for hope, I saw myself looking back at me. And when I realized that because of where I had gone to school and how I spoke, these young people had no idea that I had once been in their exact situations, I realized it was time for me to integrate all of the parts of myself so that I could be of service. I realized that though I was still very much in process, I had survived. I had overcome. Now my responsibility and privilege was to be about the survival and overcoming of others.

This decision to integrate the various parts of myself required me to be very honest with myself and with others. And this honesty deepened my healing. I discovered that a part of me (old thoughts and feelings) still worried that I was destined to fail. I realized that a part of me (old thoughts and feelings) still felt like I was an imposter who would be found out—that I didn't deserve the success I had achieved.

There is nothing like helping someone else work through the issues you have dealt with to help you clarify your healing around those issues. I could not tell my students that the thoughts they were holding about themselves and their futures were false and then ignore the moments when those same thoughts arose for me. My investment in my students' healing solidified and deepened my own.

Purpose is the bridge past ego.

Purpose is the bridge past ego. I define ego as both a person's insecurities and conceits about him- or herself in the world. Ego lives in the realm of thoughts and feelings. And when we exist in the space of ego, we are operating as if our thoughts and feelings are absolute truths rather than children of our Authentic Self who can be "raised" to be productive, positively contributing members of our lives. Ego says, "I will never be good enough," or "I am better than someone else." The Authentic Self says, "You are the unlimited potential to create, do, or be anything. *And* so is everyone."

Purpose lives in the realm of the Authentic Self. Purpose lives in the space of unlimited possibility and our interconnectedness to one another. Purpose says, "In our deepest core, there is no separation between who I am and who you are. We are all the unlimited potential to create, do, or be *anything*." Purpose asks the question "What can I give?" And this question immediately takes us out of our thoughts and feelings and into a space of seeing ourselves as agents of change and transformation. In this way, purpose is the bridge past ego. Our purpose becomes the bridge over our limiting thoughts and feelings.

HOW DO I IDENTIFY MY PURPOSE?

Many people ask, "But how do I identify my purpose? I don't even know where to begin." This chapter will conclude with a detailed exercise to help you identify and clarify your purpose. But let's first explore some core concepts that will assist the process.

As we just began to explore, clarifying purpose requires you to ask the question, "What can I give?" What do you know you do well? What have you survived? What do you know that you know in the very marrow of your bones? What is so unique about you and your life's journey that you could write a dissertation on it? What are the issues you face that no matter how much you grow, these issues continue to resurface in moments of insecurity or vulnerability?

> When we help others
> through their pain,
> we solidify our own healing.

We are all wounded healers. We are always in the process of healing and evolving no matter how far we've come. And often our deepest pain is the path to our highest purpose. Often the very issues we have wrestled with time and time again are the issues we can assist others with healing through. Why? In our efforts to overcome and sometimes just survive an issue, it's almost like we develop a Ph.D. on the subject. We read books. We have long conversations with others who have been through the same situation. We light up when we come across a movie, television show, article, or song that discusses the issue. We feel affirmed and that we are not alone. This level of identification with a particular issue can be useful when viewed through the lens of the Authentic Self. I am not speaking of being trapped in a cycle of past pain and confusion. I am speaking of knowing your Authentic Self and, from that space of unlimited possibility, owning and celebrating what you have survived, in an effort to be of service to others. And the greatest discovery is that when we help others through their pain we solidify our own healing. Your purpose may be rooted in experiences in your life, but it will ultimately be about being of service to others.

WHAT LOOKS LIKE A DISASTER MIGHT BE A DIRECTION

Sometimes purpose evolves over time. And sometimes what looks like a disaster is actually a direction. People have said to me, "But I'm a mess, I'm not ready to think about helping someone else. I need to get myself together." First of all, you are not a mess. That is a lie you have told yourself, and now you have the tools to breathe, observe that thought, and replace it with one that empowers you. "I am healing and evolving. I am better today than I was yesterday!" And secondly, no matter where you may stand in this moment, there is almost certainly someone who stands behind you. By this I mean, there is someone who is less far along his or her path than you are. And having the courage to be generous with yourself and others about your small victories, while at the same time being honest with yourself and others about what you are still going through, can be very empowering. Think about it, how much easier is it to relate to people who are being real about both their victories and areas of growth? And how many times have we seen people pretend as though they have it all figured out, and we inevitably discover they have wounded places like everyone else? No matter where you feel you are in your healing journey, you have something to give. And the very place you feel most insecure might be a clue to your purpose.

SOMETIMES PURPOSE TAKES YOU OUT OF YOUR COMFORT ZONE

The familiar can be very comfortable. But if we do what we have always done we will most likely get what we have always gotten. Again, purpose is a bridge that stretches us outside ourselves. To clarify and live in purpose, we have to get comfortable with being uncomfortable. We will be challenged to enter new arenas, be leaders, and speak with confidence about how we perceive the world. Others may not immediately understand or agree with our vision of what we would like to create. Sometimes we will have to shift resources from one place to another or ask for support. All of these aspects of embracing our purpose and more can make us uncomfortable. Still, taking a first step in the direction of your purpose leads you to the next step and so on and so on. And you may very well discover that you are more equipped to execute your purpose than you ever imagined. You just may discover that everything that has been happening in your life has been leading you toward your purpose.

At first living in your purpose may be challenging, and you will not always be able to judge your purpose by your circumstances. Sometimes there is a process of development and transformation. For example, if you decide you want to change careers, there may be a period of time when you have to get new training or even go back to school. There is a possibility that you will have to take a pay cut or not see friends as often. You may have to work very, very long hours to manifest this new dream. During this process of development, you may feel fatigued, frustrated, disconnected from what you really want.

But ultimately, there will be a flow. You will know you are in your purpose when the provision just starts falling. Things that you could not make happen on your own just start happening. You will learn the new skills necessary to step into the new phase of your life. Your gifts and genuine passion will carve a place for you in the world, especially if you remain tenacious in connecting to your passion. Think about how infectious it is to hear people speak about their work when they truly love what they do. Moving toward your dreams with passion and clarity will enable you to find allies. Sometimes these allies may just have a few positive words to say. Sometimes they will be able to connect you to someone in your field who can support you toward your dream. Perhaps you will encounter people who will invest time and even financial resources to help you toward your goals.

WHAT IS YOUR PASSION?

Purpose is often connected to Passion. And often you must look at the deepest aspect of that passion. What moves you in the world? What fills you with joy? What enrages you? What do you love most about life? What do you desperately wish would change in the world? Intensity of feeling, passion, is a wonderful way to begin to identify one's purpose.

In my healing journey, every time I saw a film or television program that featured a father and son working through their relationship, I was deeply moved. I remember while I was a student at Yale, coming into New York City and going to see Spike Lee's movie *He Got Game*, about a recently incarcerated father working through his relationship with his son. I was sitting with a friend, and by about midway through the movie, I was a total wreck. I moved a couple of rows up to try to hide the tears that were turning into full body convulsions. Eventually, I left the movie theater, went into a bathroom stall, and wept.

To this day, after all of the work I have done on my healing around my father's abandonment, when I see a similar story I am still deeply moved. Today, I no longer cry tears of sorrow, but I am still very affected. When I see a father walking with his child on his shoulders or playing with his children in the park my heart lights up. When I see a photograph of a father being loving and present with his children, my world is made brighter. Why? The issue of fathers being productive, loving participants in their children's lives is a core aspect of my particular purpose.

And then, I can unpack my understanding of my purpose even further. Sometimes we have to look at the deepest meaning of the story of our purpose. My deepest wound was around my father's abandonment. When I see a father being loving and present with his children, I see the possibility of my deepest wound healed. So while a particular aspect of my purpose is fathers and children, the larger story of my purpose is that I believe in the possibility of people healing their deepest wounds and living present and loving lives.

PURPOSE AND SOCIAL JUSTICE

One powerful expression of purpose is to stand up and speak out for social justice and societal change. The greatest possibility for justice is the discovery that there is no separation between ourselves and others. When we truly understand this, we discover that when anyone is suffering we are all in pain. And understanding this truth is crucial to creating the coalitions necessary to address the socioeconomic disparities facing our nation and our world. Consider this poem from my musical *Tearing Down the Walls.*

It's late and we're late.
And I'm starting to wonder if we'll ever be on time.
It's time for change but we are getting left behind.
They say pain don't last always
But this pain it won't subside.
People open your mouths, we're running out of time.
Who cries for the ones who have lost their voice,
And worse yet, who do not realize they are mute?
Choked silent by cycles of poverty and neglect
The only sounds they make are repetitious cries
Disguised as keeping it real or what it takes to get by.
Buy my people some awareness so we can open our ears
         and hear
Our utterings are painful to those who have gone before
And woefully absent of direction for those yet to come
Come open your throats and if you must cry,
Let it be a cry of liberation to break this shallow foundation
         we call existence
And spring forth Ancestral roots of courage and overcoming
To remind us of the truth of who we are.
Our voices are glorious
Give them breath and sing out.
Sing out raw, urgent, and bold.

Sing out for the Ancestors who only have voice through you.
Sing out for our children who need direction and do not
    know their true sound.
Sing out for those who have lost their voice and do not know
    that they are mute.

Who cries for those who have lost their voice and do not realize they are mute? Who cries for the children? Who cries for those who are poor, disenfranchised, and without hope? Who cries for those who are so lost in the maze of their negative thoughts and emotions that they cannot even see the possibility of peace and joy? We do. When we become truly present with our Authentic Self, we have no choice but to speak out and imagine new possibilities for those in need.

EXERCISE:
Discovering and Defining Purpose

Purpose is defined as an object to be reached; a target; an aim; a goal; a result that is desired; an intention. My purpose is to inspire people to transform their pain into power. I do this through the lens of my experience as an African-American man. Through my knowing my Authentic Self and choosing to be bold and open about the specificity of my journey, my work becomes universal and has the possibility of reaching all people. Universality comes through truth and specificity. The more truthful and specific I am about my experience, the more vivid that experience becomes to others—and I increase the possibility that others will be able to relate.

Take out your notebook, go to your quiet place, and answer the following questions:

1. What did you love to do most as a child?

   What brings you the most joy in the world?

   What moves you the most when you witness it in your life, on television, in the movies?

   What enrages you?

   What are your specific gifts—what do you know you do well, and no one can convince you otherwise?

   If you could have an impact on the lives of one particular group of people, who would that be and why?

2. Now answer the following Statements of Purpose:

   My purpose is to inspire/motivate/provoke (who?) _____

   _____

   To transform/understand/become (what?) _____

   _____

Once you have answered these questions around your purpose, I invite you to revisit them daily for at least a week. Each time you review them, ask yourself, "Is this the truest, highest expression of my purpose? What words or phrases could I shift to make this purpose more clear and specific and bold?" As you review your responses, also begin to dream about what your life would look like if you lived in this purpose. What would your job be? Who would be your closest advisors and friends? What training might you need? What aspects of your life would need to change to make this purpose a reality?

Clarifying one's purpose can lead to major life changes, so I ask you to be gentle and patient with yourself during this process. I also encourage you to review your Affirmations and Manifesto to remind yourself of all the tremendous work you have done and how much power you truly have to live in your purpose. The world needs all of us to live as fully in our purpose as we can. We each enter this world with unique gifts. Our lives provide us with experiences to deepen and refine those gifts. It then becomes our responsibility and our privilege to clarify our purpose so that we can give those gifts to the world.

10

The Power of Patience and Tenacity

BIRTHIN' PAINS

All of these birthin' pains and you tell me to push again?
All of these birthin' pains and you tell me to push again?
I—aaaaahhh!—don't wanna push no more!
Don't wanna push no more!

So many days on this journey—I'm still not there.
My heart, it screams, but no one seems to care.
I lay tossin' and turnin' until my body says no
Then a voice inside says, baby, push some mo'.

Been knocked down so often I've gotten used to the floor.
And I just wanna lay down here, don't wanna push no more.
But a voice inside says, if you wanna be free
You gotta get up, you gotta push not sleep.

But my energy's spent, and there's no hope at the bank,
I gave it my best shot and now I'm drawing a blank.
But that voice inside says, you are more than you dream.
Push some more, things are not what they seem.

Well, if I push again, you've got to meet me halfway
'Cause my heart is limpin' from these cripplin' days
And that voice inside says, push beyond what you feel
Dig deep inside and find the strength to heal.

'Cause through your pain you will make a new you
You gotta push and roll it until the makin's through.
And the day will come when you will look back
And say I thought I was lost, but I was right on track.

had clarified my purpose, but the process of implementing it would not be an easy one. I decided I wanted to tell stories that explored the pain of people living on the fringes of society and show them overcoming the challenges of race, class, and injustice to manifest lives of power and joy. I wanted to tell stories of people transforming their pain to power.

I had trained at different points in my studies as an actor, singer, and writer, but I was unclear of how to put these various pieces together. I began to meditate on the idea of freedom. What does it mean to be free? After all, most of my life I had felt bound—bound by my past pain and incapable of moving beyond it. And now that I was having an experience of freedom—being able to experience joy and create a healthy, balanced life—I wanted to explore it in all its facets. What are the barriers to freedom—freedom to dream, to have possibility and hope? How could more people experience freedom?

I began to write solo plays exploring these themes. At this point, I still did not have an agent. I mailed literally hundreds of letters and head shots to agents in hopes they would represent me. I did this for years and never received one response. Once I had completed a play, I mailed or e-mailed copies to literally hundreds of theaters and festivals around the country and never received a single response.

Well, there is an expression: "If you can't find a door, build a door." When it became clear to me that I wasn't going to be able to enter through the traditional doors of the entertainment industry, I decided I needed to build my own door with the minimal resources I had as a teaching artist and with the help of friends. Besides, I knew I was endeavoring to tell stories of people whose voices had often been muted, and I felt a conviction to make them finally be heard.

I would start with small presentations of my plays for four or five friends at a friend's home. And when those friends responded favorably, I would ask them to tell their friends. Eventually, I had a small group of friends and friends of friends who were interested in what I had to say.

So then I would rent a small space and invite anyone I knew to come for free to see me perform. When I look back, I marvel at how determined and slightly insane I was. Because my plays told stories of people often on the fringes of society, I would e-mail and call affiliate nonprofits working with young people, the homeless, people dealing with substance abuse, and the formerly incarcerated and tell them what I was doing and invite them to attend. Little by little people began to show up. I was patient (albeit, reluctantly) and I was tenacious. I refused to give up.

This beginning phase of my professional career also mirrored the evolution of my healing journey. At this point, I had been in therapy, tried various religions, done a handful of healing and empowerment workshops, and read every self-help and spiritual book you could imagine. I had unpacked my pain and was actively in the process of living in the present and creating an empowered future. Still, I had periods when I would forget how much I had healed and overcome, especially in the face of working so hard to make my dreams come true and all the rejection along the path. I had periods when the old, negative thoughts and feelings would reemerge. "See, you are destined to fail. You haven't healed, you are just pretending." I had to fight like hell to maintain my sanity and belief in my own possibility. And honestly, sometimes I would forget. I would become impatient with the process. But, somehow, I would always remember to remember and try again. I would remember to remember all I had learned in the books I had read and the words of the various mentors, friends, and spiritual leaders who had advised me. And I would try again . . . patience and tenacity. Eventually, I noticed a pattern. Sure, I would get discouraged and forget the truth of who I was and the purpose to which I was committed, but those periods were becoming shorter and fewer. Sure, I would still have days when I questioned if I could ever experience true happiness in my life on a consistent basis or if I would ever have a platform for my purpose, but those periods were becoming shorter and fewer.

I had developed an abundance of tools both in my profession and in my healing journey, and I continued to study and learn more and more. Eventually, I came to realize that I was okay— that wellness was the norm. Sure, I had/have moments of doubt and discouragement, but I began to see them for just that . . . moments . . . thoughts . . . thoughts that I could systematically, continually replace with new, empowering thoughts.

And similarly, this practice of patience and tenacity has opened doors of opportunity for me to express my purpose greater than my wildest dreams. It has been more than a decade since I completed graduate school and even longer since I began my Healing Journey. And the process has taught me the power of patience and tenacity.

Healing and manifesting the lives of our dreams requires a healthy balance of both Patience and Tenacity. Sometimes the journey to transform our pain to power is a day-by-day, often moment-by-moment process. At times, the level of consciousness required to be present with our Authentic Self can be tedious. Yet I am a firm believer that the absence of presence with our Authentic Self is a much harder way of life. Still the absence of presence is what is familiar to most of us (being lost in the maze of our negative thoughts and emotions). The absence of presence is the way much of the world lives. The choice to be our best selves, to be present and intentional in our lives requires the POWER OF PATIENCE AND TENACITY.

> PATIENCE is the internal choice to know you are moving in the direction of your dreams even when external circumstances don't always affirm it.

I am often reluctantly patient, but patient nonetheless. I say reluctantly patient because a part of me didn't want to and still doesn't want to wait for the things I desire in my life and for the world. A part of me felt and feels like I already wasted too much of my life in sadness and insecurity, and now that I know who I am, I want to remember and live in the power of that knowing every moment of every day. But the reality is we all forget sometimes. The reality is that though there are moments of flow in our lives when everything just seems to happen exactly as we desire, in the perfect timing we've laid out, there are also moments when we have to be patient. And being impatient only causes us pain. So I define patience as the internal choice to know we are moving in the direction of our dreams even when external circumstances don't always affirm it. Patience is the choice to be present with our Authentic Self.

Impatience is only thoughts of limitation and fear of lack. Impatience is only the limiting thought that time is running out or that obtaining certain things or having a relationship with a particular person will create happiness. Impatience is only the feeling of fear that the imagined happiness of having that thing or being in a relationship with that person will never be obtained. True happiness is presence with the Authentic Self. True happiness is the choice to be present in this very moment where there is nothing to be fixed, obtained, or discarded. And from the space of this truth we can play the game of obtaining things or having relationships with people, not as the source of our happiness, but as an extension of our unlimited possibility to create, do, or be *anything.*

> TENACITY is the choice to be determined and persistent about being present with your Authentic Self and creating the life of your dreams regardless of the work and focus it may require.

Are you tenacious? Are you willing to push beyond past pain and limiting thoughts and feelings once and for all? Are you willing to do what it takes to have the life of your dreams? I firmly believe that we can manifest our greatest dreams through presence with our Authentic Self, but we must exercise the muscle of tenacity. When past pain and familiar negative thoughts emerge, we have to be tenacious about feeding ourselves empowering thoughts and feelings. When the myriad of triggers happen in our lives that cause us to forget the truth of who we are, we must be tenacious about remembering to remember. We must remember to Breathe, to Observe, to Choose, to be Intentional, to Create.

There comes a time when we must press past the pain of our

past experiences. We must press past the pain of negative inheritances. We must decide once and for all to be victorious.

We must remember to Breathe,
to Observe, to Choose,
to be Intentional, to Create.

Decide that you are willing to pay the price. Decide: I'm not going down; I'm going through. Sometimes if your life has been full of enough challenges and disappointments, you may question if things will ever change. But you must make up your mind that you are not going to quit. You are not going to give up. If you can't say anything for a while but "I'm still here!" That is a victory—that is the power of tenacity.

Consider this exploration of the Power of Tenacity in my poem "Push the Rock."

Push the Rock

It happened about a year ago, I awoke with something blocking my view.
I could tell there was a problem because usually the sun shines through.
I went to my window and saw darkness staring straight at me:
Not the sun, not the sky, not even a tree.
And so I said, "God, what's going on? Savior, this can't be.

I have a full day planned—places to go, people to see."

And God said, "Not today. Open your door—take a peek."

And what I saw was so bizarre it made my knees a little
*   weak.*

There was this huge rock in front of my door:

20 feet wide by 20 feet tall, maybe even more.

If I was ever going to leave my house, this rock could
*   never stay*

And since I knew I couldn't move it by myself, I began
*   to pray:*

"God, why is this huge rock messing up my life?

I have things to do—I don't have time for all this strife."

And God said, "Push the rock. That's all I ask of you.

This is my plan. There is nothing more to do."

So I began to push, pushed all morning and through the
*   night,*

Dug my feet into the ground, pushed with all my might.

But that rock did not move an inch

I was getting hostile and my teeth began to clench:

"God, You see me pushing this rock! Can't you help a
*   brother out?"*

And God said, "Push the rock. Trust in me. Don't doubt."

Well, the next morning when I awoke, that rock was still
*   there:*

"God, why have you forsaken me? Why won't you answer my
*   prayer?"*

And God said, "Push the rock. That is all I ask of you.

This is my plan. There is nothing more to do."
For a long time I fought it, thinking if I complained enough
God would see this rock's too big—He's being way too tough.
I began to push, pushed for days, weeks, months, a year,
Went through every emotion: rage, pain, sorrow, fear;
"People say You're all knowing, well I'm starting to have my
     doubts;
If I were running things, I'd let a brother leave his house!"
Then just last week I awoke with light blaring in my eye.
It was like a dream to see the sun, the trees, the sky:
"God, what happened, you decided to have mercy on me?"
And God said, "Son, it was never a question of mercy, but of
     maturity.
How often have you ignored the beauty of nature or the
     grace to go about your day?
Now when you see the sun you will know it is because God
     has made a way.
You thought the rock was punishment for something you'd
     done wrong.
The rock was a gift, my child, a gift sent to make you strong:
Look at the muscles in your arms, your chest, your legs, your
     hands.
Don't you know, I am the Lord your God? Nothing is hap-
     penstance.
Afraid of the unknown, you constantly try to grasp control.
Plan your life out perfectly, moving boldly towards your goal.
But I can take you higher than you can climb alone.

Only God remains when all earthly pursuits are gone.
Look at yourself, my son, see how much you've grown.
If I hadn't sent this rock, you would have never known
How blessed you are, the abundant plans I have for you:
There is battle raging, I need warriors: I am calling you."
What rock stands in your life that you are trying desperately
    to resist?
No matter how much you fast and pray this rock seems to
    persist?
Perhaps the blessing is in the pushing,
God's plan to build new strength in you—
Perhaps what God wants for your life
Is greater than that what you had planned to do—
God said, "Push the rock."

The very challenges you worried might overwhelm you have actually formed you into the survivor, the overcomer you are. The boulders of doubt, insecurity, and lack that have blocked the light of joy in your life have only made you stronger and given you a story to tell. You are a survivor. You are an overcomer. You are the unlimited potential to create, do, or be *anything*!

STATEMENTS OF AFFIRMATION

Throughout the previous chapters, I have provided you with numerous models of Statements of Affirmation and even provided prompts for you to create your own. The task now is to review the various Statements of Affirmation provided in this book as well as the ones you have begun to create for yourself. Create a document for yourself of the Statements of Affirmation that cause you to feel the most empowered and proclaim them daily. As your dreams for your life continue to clarify, adjust them accordingly. You now have the tools necessary to create your reality through presence with your Authentic Self and the power of Affirmative Speaking.

11

The Power of Your Environment

O nce you are clear about the power of your Authentic Self, about the life you choose to create for yourself, and about what you are committed to giving to others, you must protect this clarity at all cost. The POWER OF YOUR ENVIRONMENT is a crucial aspect in maintaining presence with your Authentic Self and being intentional in your life. By environment, I mean not only the people with whom you surround yourself, but the thoughts and images you allow to enter into your psyche through media.

WHO IS IN YOUR INNER CIRCLE?

If you want to evaluate the condition of your life, examine who is in your inner circle. Once you are clear about your core values, it is imperative that you surround yourself with people who mirror those values. When you surround yourself with people who are living in the truth of their Authentic Self you have mirrors to hold you accountable and uplift you in those inevitable moments when you forget the truth of who you are.

Now, there are times when you are actively endeavoring to empower someone else to discover and know the truth of who they are. Empowering others is both the gift and the responsibility of becoming present with your Authentic Self. However, it is important to give out of your overflow and not your storehouse. When we are overflowing with clarity and joy about who we are and practicing tools on a daily basis to help us remember the truth of our Authentic Self, we are less likely to forget that truth when empowering others.

Years ago I discovered a technique to assist in this process of empowering people to know their Authentic Self. It was the summer of 1997, and I was in the very beginning of my Healing Journey. I was absolutely miserable, and this misery filled many of my conversations. I had received a contract to perform in Italy that summer singing concerts of classical music with a few other American vocalists. One soprano who was also on that tour became a dear friend and did her best to support me through this very painful period of my life. I remember one day we were standing in the center of a piazza in Florence and I was telling her one of my stories of woe about my life. At one point, I stopped myself and said, "I'm sorry, I feel like I'm weighing you down with all my baggage." She responded, "No, I'm setting your baggage right here beside me."

She was crystal clear that while she was committed to being a friend and supporting me in the process of my healing, she was absolutely not committed to carrying my baggage or personalizing my sadness.

It is possible to be a support for other people without allowing them to bring you down. As they unload, just set their baggage beside you—don't carry it. And most important, hold the space of knowing the truth of who they are—who we all are: the unlimited potential to create, do, or be *anything*.

KNOWING WHEN TO SHIFT YOUR ENVIRONMENT

When you become fully committed to living in the truth of your Authentic Self, some people in your environment will inevitably shift—they will either transform, fade away, or you may have to set a boundary on your relationship. You cannot make people around you want what they do not want. Sometimes we must separate ourselves from negative experiences and people for our own good. Be careful who is in your inner circle. You want people to honor your deepest purpose rather than allow them to manipulate you to be who they need you to be. One simple technique is to take an inventory of each person who plays a crucial role in your life and ask yourself, "How do I feel when I am in this person's presence? Do I feel joyous and empowered? If not, why?" Once you are clear about the people and relationships that impact you negatively, you must ask yourself, "What role do I play in the state of this relationship? Can it be saved? What will it cost me to save/repair it? Is this relationship valuable enough for me to repair?"

Sometimes there are also relationships in which you have a responsibility to someone that you can't just cut off, like a child who is going through a difficult time or an ailing parent, friend, or mate. Still, there is always a way to set boundaries and honor yourself. Perhaps you might have to ask a friend to babysit a child or ailing friend/relative even for a few hours so you can clear your head and have some space to remember who you are. Perhaps you won't be able to get someone to change his/her behavior completely, but there may be a smaller request that would help you honor yourself and shift the environment significantly.

Some people can sit in the front row of your life, some in the balcony. And then there are others who you can't even let into the theater. In fact, you might need a restraining order.

Our environments can have a tremendous impact on our state of being. Think about the people with whom you consistently spend time. Inevitably, someone will come to mind that no matter how good you are feeling before you spend time with that person, he or she will bring you down. Often, it is not intentional on the person's part. Sometimes people can be so committed to their misery it becomes infectious. Now, I am not at all suggesting that we turn our backs on people we care about who are in pain.

Sometimes we all need support and a listening ear. However, there are some people who are so committed to their pain that no amount of support or listening can shift them. You have to know what is acceptable behavior for you and be vigilant in your determination to protect your peace of mind and positive emotions.

THE POWER OF ENTERTAINMENT

VISION

Where there is no vision a people will perish
So we must embrace a vision that will give us life
We celebrate that change has come to the White House
We cannot underestimate the soul transforming power of this
vision—
Not only for ourselves but for our children—
The vision not only of President Obama, but the entire first
family:
Thank God a change has come,
And we also acknowledge that more of our children watch
BET than CNN.
We are all family here, so let's speak the truth . . .
Our American entertainment still needs a Civil Rights
Movement.
If you want to control the psyche of a people control the way
they perceive themselves.

Create little black boxes and large screens
Where we parade about as though ignorant of our dignity.
Where our women are displayed as whores and our men as
  angry beasts.
Put in lots of loud music with steady hard beats
And throw in some bling bling for bad taste.
I am not angry.
I am enraged.
Enraged enough to remember, to honor, to create:
To refuse to write black tragedy—too many of our lives have
  been tragic enough
But to tell a story of possibility and hope—
We must tell a story the empowers our village from coast to
  coast and across waters.
We must tell a story that proclaims: some may not see you,
  but I know you are beautiful.
We must tell a story that provides the affirmation we all need
  to know we are not insane.
In a world where we are losing jobs and losing homes and
  losing hope,
In a time where degrading images pervade our airways,
In an America where one in three of our black boys will
  spend time in prison,
And HIV/AIDS is the number one killer of young black
  women—
We need to tell a new story, the true story like never before—
The charge is ours:

To be more brilliant than we ever dreamed we could
To value our lives when others do not
To clap our hands and give that unmistakable Amen of
*   affirmation*
To tell the story that will free our sons, fathers, brothers from
*   prison*
The story that will give our sisters, daughters, mothers long
*   overdue moments of rest.*
The story that shatters the crack pipe,
Erases illiteracy, depression, and ignorance,
And obliterates every lie that has ever been told about our
*   intelligence and our beauty.*
It is time to tell a new story, the true story—
We must tell the story for ourselves and for our children.

I believe the greatest way to control the possibility of a people is to control the way they see themselves—see their possibility, see their futures. They say the eyes are the windows to the soul. What we view with our eyes gets into our souls. The Bible teaches us that faith comes by hearing, but it's also true that a negative self-image and the resulting negative emotions also come by hearing. Have you ever had an experience of listening to a song when you first wake up in the morning or on your drive to work and that same song plays in your mind throughout the day? You may lie down to rest at night and that same song is still playing in your mind. Music is mantra. It gets in the soul. We must become more aware of the impact that our "entertainment" has on us.

CONNECT RECONNECT

I was born in the ghetto
In a cold violent town
And just like the ghetto
My soul is feeling worn down,
It's been a long, a long time comin'
But I know a change is gonna come—
When we connect disconnect connect reconnect connect
connect connect.
As I teach my students in class, we hear a loud Bang!
They immediately duck and I stand in shock as a man lies slain
On the block in front of our school—
And I think to myself . . .
As our superstars bling bling our children dodge bullets
Inside of schools too old and worn down for their brilliance
So they embrace a life that's all their own
Full of the beat that's beating them down
Unconscious of the truth that it's an ancient beat that's been
passed down
Full of the pain and promise of their progenitors
Pulsating through their blood and feet as they walk.
Connect disconnect connect reconnect
As I stare into my students' faces and I see the past,
A past too brilliant for them to even comprehend but true
none the less.

As thirteen-year-old LaDre tells LaQuisha to "move b** get
out the way"
I tell them of the architectural genius of those definitively
dark-skinned Egyptians
Who gave astronomy, mathematics, literature
Long before classical Greece started training for the Olympics.
But can they hear me?
'Cause Disney, he's been lying to our children,
Prince of Egypt got it wrong.
Put some chocolate in those crayons, Walt, and we can all get
along.
But this poem is not about blaming the man
Black Superstar, tell me, where do you stand?
Are you standing at all as our children fall
Into the depths of despair? Are you there?
Bling bling? Oh, now I've got your attention.
I hold you in poetic detention until you learn this lesson:
Our children will watch BET and buy your CD
Before they will ever think of reading a book
So as you sip Courvoisier think of the knowledge you took
Out of a brilliant young mind, you know it's a crime
And you ought to be fined on every dollar you make
Make no mistake as you sit and chew steak—a starving
black child paid for it
You are profiting off of our children's neglect
Put some thought in your lyrics and show some respect

Words are powerful, you have endless effect
So get over yourself and choose to connect
To something greater than your own ego
And let our children know you care, I swear
I wish I could sell all your gold chains, diamond rings, and
*   big cars*
And build better schools in the ghetto and make our children
*   our stars*
Artist? You are blessed with an ancient gift
You have hearts to inspire and souls to lift
Heal the psychic scars festering on the minds of our people.
Say it from the mic, from the court, from the highest church
*   steeple:*
We are more than some think we are!
We are more than we think we are!
Besides the b-ball and the football,
Now the tennis and the golf balls,
In education and finances they done cut off our—
And in case you want to file my words under bitter pessimist
Let me take a moment to suggest that none of us is free when
*   our babies are oppressed.*
And though some of us might make it, can we collectively
*   succeed*
When our future's being devastated, when our children can
*   hardly read?*
When most of them have no idea or worse the wrong idea
Of who we were and therefore are and might be.

Give MacDaddy some trigonometry, teach Hoochie some
  French,
Make Bebe and Shenene attorneys for the defense,
For the defense of our dignity,
For the defense of our pride,
Get crunk with the truth 'cause His-Story is a lie!
It's been a long time comin' but a change is gonna come
A change is gonna come, a change is gonna come
When we connect reconnect reconnect reconnect
For our children!

Everything has either a positive or a negative vibration. What is the usefulness of base entertainment that appeals to the lowest aspects of who we are—arguing, materialism, repetitions of confusion? What is the point? Why is this considered dramatic or interesting? Why this fascination with, celebration of, a repetition of our pain? Our children are being dropped every day, but when are we going to start to explore the real reasons why that is happening and begin to hold up models and images of how we can uplift ourselves and our children?

ENTERTAINMENT AND THE AFRICAN-AMERICAN COMMUNITY

As an African-American working in the entertainment industry, I firmly believe our entertainment must speak to the myriad of complex, urgent, and painful issues facing the African-American community and thereby our nation as a whole.

If we really want to explore the pain, we need to go to the root. Not as excuse making, but so some real healing can take place. What is the root of the breakdown of our families? Why are so many of our fathers absent and so many single mothers worn out and frustrated? Let's tell the truth of the negative aspects of our Cultural Inheritance—the legacy of slavery and disenfranchisement in this country—so we can be real about what we must do to heal. In my play *Through the Night*, a single black mother talks about the emotions surrounding her raising a black boy in this society.

> *You want to know why I'm so angry?*
> *It's been bubbling in my DNA for centuries—*
> *Ever since they sold away my man from me—*
> *And he been having trouble finding his way home ever since.*
> *And every time I look at my son I see his father's face*
> *And I have to remember I love my son—*
> *It's his trifling daddy I hate love hate—*
> *You try raising a black boy in this society—playing mom*
>   *and dad—*
> *It ain't no joke—hell yeah, I'm mad—*
> *And if you cross me, I'm gone let you know it too—*
> *You want me to be nice and gentle?*
> *Then take half this work I got to do—*

Yes, I will place my hand on my hips, smack lips and roll
  my neck
'Cause my black boy's gone make it

In this play I also show a community of black men being fathers and mentors, sometimes hurting, but ultimately loving the women in their lives. They make mistakes, have flaws, but ultimately they are fighting to overcome. Our healing can be dramatic. It must be because . . .

"Our children are watching,
And when they see us crumbling it gives them reason not to
  build,
When they see us dying reason not to live,
Our children are watching."

What's the end game? Our children must be protected. Our families must heal. Explorations of our pain are only useful as a pathway to our healing. And we must tell the truth. For me, one aspect of this truth is honoring the dynamic, powerful role black women have played in the face of the trauma and pain the larger community has experienced. Black women have often loved black men more than we have been able to love ourselves.

Why? Because they know there are roots to our brokenness that are much deeper than our actions too often display. They know there are black men fighting to beat the odds—the statistics—and succeeding every day. And they know that even though too often our behaviors may belie it, black men do love black women. We must do better, and I am a firm believer that this must be done through images that remind us of our greatest possibility. And sometimes we must learn to celebrate the greatness of the everyday black man who is present in the home and endeavoring to be responsible to his wife and his children. Consider this next passage from my play *Through the Night*. Sarah is the speaker. Her husband owns a health food store in the heart of an urban neighborhood, and he is the principal caregiver for their child while Sarah works long hours. Because the business has not been successful, Sarah's husband is feeling insecure. Consider how she celebrates him:

> *A black man needs something he owns*
> *To overcome a history of being property—*
> *I'm tired from being on my feet all day,*
> *But I'll stay on my feet because I believe in him.*
> *I believe in his dream.*
> *He cannot close down this shop.*
> *He's my King.*
> *He's not so grand,*
> *But he's my stand-up black man.*
> *Consistent and always there,*
> *He's an answer to my prayer—*
> *In school he got mostly B's and C's,*
> *But he's straight A's with me,*

He may not be the finest man in the room,
But when I walk away I know I can assume,
His eyes are following me—
He's the kind of man I want our son to be,
He cannot close down this shop.
He's a strong man,
But sometimes strong men feel weak:
So last night I held him and he wept—
No words were spoken—no need.
And somehow I love him more.
And the love is so wide I climb deep inside and I am
  renewed
That's why I'm putting on these pumps and heading back
  to work

Regardless of how much pain we have experienced or how broken our environments may seem, we can and must heal. This healing can begin with a single individual—this healing can begin with you. If your current environment is in opposition to this healing, you may first have to disconnect in order to take care of yourself, but there is always a possibility of reaching back for those you love. Or perhaps you won't have to totally disconnect, and you can just find moments and spaces to make your healing a priority. Either way, you must be very aware of your environment and how it is impacting you—we must protect our knowledge of the truth of our Authentic Self at all costs.

Creating a new environment that fosters healing and that

honors your highest purpose can at times be painful. You may lose long-held relationships, but new ones will emerge. You have the power to decide who and what you will allow to be a part of your life. I encourage you to review your Manifesto, your Affirmations, and your Statements of Purpose as you contemplate changes you may wish to make to your environment. Our environments (the people with whom we surround ourselves and the media we choose to perceive) can have tremendous impact on our thoughts, feelings, and ultimately behavior.

12

The Power of Joy

Row, row, row your boat gently down the stream,
Merrily, merrily, merrily, merrily life is but a dream . . .

—TRADITIONAL NURSERY RHYME

There is a tremendous amount of wisdom in this traditional nursery rhyme, and I believe it holds the secret to the POWER OF JOY.

JOY is the choice to be happy.

Happiness is a choice. As I've shared in the previous chapters, for much of my life I believed that joy would never be a possibility for me. Today, my life is full of joy. Not because everything is perfect or works out the way I want it to, but because I finally understand that I can choose joy at any moment in my life regardless of the circumstances surrounding me. And this nursery rhyme will help me illustrate this point.

Row, row, row your boat gently down the stream . . .

The boat is a metaphor for one's life. Rowing is a practice that requires precision (specificity of action and intentionality). In this nursery rhyme, the task of rowing is repeated three times, suggesting that one must continually row, which makes sense—if you only row a boat once, you will not get very far. And the instruction is to row gently—to be easy with the process of this precise, sometimes challenging task of rowing.

This is the perfect parallel to the process of choosing to be present with the Authentic Self. It is a practice that requires precision (specificity of action and intentionality). We must make the choice, often moment by moment, to observe what we are thinking and feeling, and then choose thoughts and feelings that empower rather than limit us. We must remember all that we have inherited, and then choose to be intentional about employing what works for us, and discarding familiar patterns that only limit us. We must choose once and for all to forgive, have faith, be tenacious, live on purpose, and protect our environment. And we must continually row, row, row the boat of our lives, meaning we must daily, sometimes moment by moment, make the choice to be intentional and create the life of our dreams. And because this process can be challenging, we must constantly choose to be gentle with ourselves. And the result of these choices . . .

Merrily, merrily, merrily, merrily life is but a dream . . .

Just as the row is repeated three times, the merrily is repeated four. The level of merriment and joy in our lives is in direct relationship to how intentional and persistent we are with the rowing of our boat. And if we forget this truth, we must simply remember to remember. We must simply breathe and become intentional once again. That's the miracle of this dream of life. At any moment, we can choose to row again and instantly joy becomes accessible to us. At any moment we can choose to breathe, observe, and steer the boat of our lives in the direction of our choosing.

Truly, life is but a dream. Life is the dream you choose it to be. Regardless of the sorrow and hardships you have faced in your life, you have the power to choose joy. Congratulations. You have done the work. You now have the tools to transform your pain to power. Now you must simply row, row, row. And may your life be filled with boundless joy.

Row, row, row your boat gently down the stream,
Merrily, merrily, merrily, merrily life is but a dream . . .